BRINGING IT **HOME** PRESENTS

Entertaining at Home with
America's Top Chefs

pil

Publications International, Ltd.

Front cover photography and photography on pages 13, 21, 23, 25, 26, 35, 39, 45, 85, 87, 89, 119, 139, 169 and 179 by Chris Cassidy Photography, Inc.

Photography on pages 79, 81, 129, 131 and 141 by Stephen Hamilton Photographics, Inc.

Pictured on the front cover: Grilled Pork Tenderloin on Wild Mushroom Potato Risotto with Chipotle Honey Drops *(page 44)*.

Pictured on the back cover (clockwise from top): Hand-Cut Ahi Tuna Tartare with Avocado, Yuzu, Mustard Oil and Black Radish *(page 34)*, Blackened Fresh Ahi Summer Rolls with Soy Ginger Sesame Sauce *(page 22)* and Grilled Kauai Shrimp and Monterey Crab Cake with Grilled Green Garlic and Grape Tomato Jus *(page 178)*.

ISBN-13: 978-1-4127-2914-7
ISBN-10: 1-4127-2914-9

Library of Congress Control Number: 2007941469

Manufactured in China.

8 7 6 5 4 3 2 1

One of my key philosophies in cooking is that the key to great-tasting recipes is great ingredients—fresh is best and the peak of freshness is even better.

I loved being a part of the cooking show *Bringing It Home* because I could demonstrate how to prepare delicious yet simple recipes using ingredients at their peak freshness. The host of the show, my friend Laura McIntosh, has made this her mission to pair great recipes with the freshest ingredients. It's no secret that when you can cook with peak-of-season fresh fruits and vegetables, you've just added the key flavor elements to great-tasting recipes. This cookbook showcases ingredients fresh from the field from some of the best chefs in America.

You will see that the recipes are simple and straightforward. The DVD included with the cookbook makes preparing them that much easier. The dishes are perfect for home entertaining where the fresh ingredients are entertainment because of their full flavor.

More and more, food aficionados are going back to their kitchens to entertain and this cookbook is just what you need to prepare great recipes at home. Whether you're entertaining your family, hosting a party, or sharing culinary delights with your friends, *Entertaining at Home with America's Top Chefs* is packed with fresh ways to make anything you cook taste great!

Enjoy,

Emeril Lagasse

80

contents

118

Recipes from Contributing Chefs

168

38

140

128

20

130

It's easy for me to explain my passion for food. I grew up in the town in Northern California where five generations of my family have farmed. During the harvest, after school and weekends were spent with my cousins in the fields. When the crops were finally in, we celebrated the bounty together with family meals in the kitchen.

My cooking show, Bringing It Home, combines this heritage with my passion for food. This cookbook is a natural next step. It is my way of sharing my vision of fresh, simple food with you.

Serving food at its best is really a simple thing if you first take the time to learn where and when food grows. Knowing when food is at its peak of freshness means we can all be great cooks because we can start with great ingredients.

Combining this simple understanding of fresh food with these amazing recipes from experienced chefs is your key to creating simple, delicious meals for your friends and family. That combination is what my show is all about, and what this cookbook highlights.

These recipes all began on Bringing It Home. The show is based on a simple premise: We bring a kitchen and a gourmet chef right out into a field ripe for harvest, and together we demonstrate what can be done with peak-of-season produce. My request of the chefs was for simple recipes that used fresh ingredients and, of course, tasted great! Then I helped them chop, slice, dice, and sauté every recipe in this book, and trust me—if these chefs can teach me to prepare these recipes, then anyone can make them, too!

The truth is, I've picked all my favorite recipes for this book. I love all of them and hope that you will too. Whether you're entertaining or simply preparing dinner for your family, I think you will find this cookbook fun, informative, and useful. In addition to new and creative recipes, it's packed full of ideas and information that I hope everyone will enjoy.

So grab an apron, pick a recipe for something in season, and let's start cooking it up nice and fresh.

Laura

Gary Arabia

Chef Gary Arabia grew up in Pittsburgh, Pennsylvania. He fell in love with cooking while watching his mother prepare family dinners in the kitchen. He set out to study various cooking styles while working his way through some of the best restaurants in the country. He is a premier caterer and event producer who brings fine dining to any special occasion.

roasted red baby bliss potato salad
with cabbage, pancetta and haricots vert

MAKES **4 SERVINGS**

3 cups red cabbage, finely sliced
3 cups green cabbage, finely sliced
8 ounces red baby bliss potatoes
  Olive oil
6 ounces thick pancetta
⅓ pound fresh green beans (haricots vert)
  Vinaigrette (recipe follows)
½ cup crumbled blue cheese

Preheat oven to 350°F. Blanch cabbage in hot water 2 minutes. Remove, drain and chill 30 minutes. Cut potatoes into ¾-inch cubes and lightly coat with olive oil. Roast in oven 25 minutes or until golden and crisp; set aside. Cut pancetta into ½-inch cubes. Sauté until crisp; set aside. Trim ends of green beans and blanch in boiling water 2 minutes; set aside. Remove cabbage from refrigerator and add potatoes, green beans, two-thirds pancetta and two-thirds blue cheese. Toss with vinaigrette and place on plate. Top with remaining pancetta and blue cheese.

Vinaigrette

6 tablespoons balsamic vinegar
2 tablespoons sherry wine vinegar
2 tablespoons Dijon mustard
1 tablespoon minced fresh thyme
2 shallots, minced
1 cup extra-virgin olive oil
⅔ cup walnut oil
½ teaspoon kosher salt
¼ teaspoon freshly ground white pepper

Whisk together vinegars, mustard, thyme and shallots. Slowly whisk in oils. When emulsified, season. Vinaigrette can be made one day ahead and refrigerated.

lobster roll
with cabbage and sweet chili dipping sauce

MAKES **4 SERVINGS**

8   large cabbage leaves
1   whole 1-pound Maine lobster
4   kaffir lime leaves, finely chopped
1   teaspoon ground cumin
¼   teaspoon kosher or sea salt
¼   teaspoon freshly ground black pepper
2   tablespoons bacon oil
    Sweet Chili Dipping Sauce (recipe
      follows)

Place cabbage leaves in steamer and steam about 8 minutes or until tender and easy to roll. Set aside. Blanch or steam lobster 3 minutes. Remove and place in ice water 5 minutes. Cut off head and tail. Clean and set aside for garnish. Remove body and claw meat. Place lobster meat in bowl and season with kaffir leaves, cumin, salt and pepper. Place lobster meat in heated bacon oil and sear 1 minute on each side. Remove lobster meat and place on towel to drain excess oil. Cut lobster meat lengthwise in half.

Place each cabbage leaf on cutting board. It should be flat and about 4×3 inches. You may overlap leaves to create desired shape. Cut off uneven ends to create rectangular shape. Place lobster meat in center of leaves and fold like a spring roll. Cut rolls into circular slices and place on center of plate, overlapping each other. Place lobster head at one end and tail at other end for presentation. Serve with sweet chili dipping sauce.

Sweet Chili Dipping Sauce
½   cup vinegar
½   teaspoon sugar
¼   teaspoon salt
2   teaspoons ground chili paste
1   teaspoon finely shredded carrots
1   teaspoon finely shredded jicama

Heat vinegar, sugar and salt and bring to a boil. Add chili paste and reduce by one-fourth. Remove and chill. Add carrots and jicama before serving.

Tony Bonacki

Chef Tony Bonacki is the Executive Chef at the Luna Park Restaurant in Los Angeles. A 15-year veteran of the food industry, Bonacki has been a chef for casual and fine dining restaurants for more than eight years.

Laura says...

To keep avocados from browning, cut them just before using or brush them with a little lemon juice.

luna park cobb salad

MAKES 4 SERVINGS

6   chicken breasts
    Cobb Chicken Marinade (recipe follows)
1   bag (12 ounces) mixed greens
1   pound cherry tomatoes, halved
8   eggs, hardboiled and crumbled
2   pounds bacon, cooked and crumbled
2   cups crumbled blue cheese
4   avocados, sliced

Marinate chicken breasts overnight, then grill until cooked through. Chop into cubes. Top lettuce bed with all salad ingredients except avocados. For traditional Cobb plating, keep ingredients in rows across lettuce. Top with sliced avocado in center. Drizzle with Blue Cheese Dressing.

Cobb Chicken Marinade

1   bunch fresh tarragon
2   bunches fresh parsley
1   bunch fresh cilantro
¾   cup fresh thyme
¾   cup fresh sage leaves
3   garlic cloves
¼   cup salt
1   tablespoon pepper
⅓   cup lemon juice
1½   cup olive oil

Combine all ingredients except olive oil in bowl of electric mixer. With mixer running, slowly add oil. Beat.

Blue Cheese Dressing

1½   shallots, minced
10   ounces blue cheese
⅓   cup sherry vinegar
1   tablespoon black pepper
1½   cups olive oil
⅔   cup extra-virgin olive oil

Combine all ingredients except olive oils in bowl of electric mixer. With mixer running, slowly add oils. Beat.

chicken achiote

with corn on the cob with chili butter
and mixed greens with lemon dressing

MAKES **8 SERVINGS**

2	ounces achiote
1½	tablespoons chopped garlic
⅔	cup tomato juice
2	tablespoons toasted and ground chile de árbol
⅓	cup whiskey
1¾	cups lemon juice
⅓	cup salt
8	half chickens
1	bag (12 ounces) mixed greens

Process achiote, garlic and tomato juice in food processor. Combine mixture with all other ingredients. Marinate chicken overnight.

Grill chicken until cooked through. Serve with Corn on the Cob with Chili Butter and mixed greens with Lemon Dressing

Corn on the Cob with Chili Butter

1	pound (4 sticks) butter
½	tablespoon red chiles, toasted and ground fine
½	cup lime juice
2	tablespoons salt
12	ears of corn, halved

Soften butter to room temperature. Combine all ingredients in mixer bowl and mix well. Bring corn just to a boil on stove, then move to grill for a few moments. Remove from heat and cover in chili butter.

Lemon Dressing

½	tablespoon salt
1½	shallots
1	cup lemon juice
2	teaspoons sugar
1	tablespoon black pepper
⅓	cup red wine vinegar
1½	cups olive oil
⅔	cup extra-virgin olive oil

Combine all ingredients except oils. With handheld blender on low speed, gradually add olive oils.

Brandon Boudet

Chef Brandon Boudet was born and raised in New Orleans. He graduated from San Francisco's California Culinary Academy and interned at K-Paul's Louisiana Kitchen and NOLA in New Orleans. Chef Boudet has worked extensively in Los Angeles and New York City. In 2004, he returned to his Italian heritage and opened Dominick's in West Hollywood, a restaurant offering a straightforward menu that rarely has more than three components to a dish.

rice balls
with roasted tomatoes & mozzarella

MAKES 4 SERVINGS

4	tomatoes, halved
1	shallot, chopped
2	tablespoons olive oil
8	ounces risotto rice
½	cup white wine
1½	cups vegetable broth
¼	cup cream
1	teaspoon fresh basil, chopped
1	teaspoon fresh parsley, chopped
1	teaspoon salt
½	teaspoon ground red pepper
1	tablespoon butter
¼	cup grated Parmesan cheese
¼	cup provolone cheese, chopped
¼	cup fresh mozzarella cheese, diced
2	eggs
2	cups milk
2	cups all-purpose flour
3	cups bread crumbs
	Vegetable oil for frying
	Salt and pepper, to taste

Preheat oven to 300°F. Season tomatoes with salt and pepper. Roast in oven 1 hour.

Sauté shallots in olive oil 3 minutes. Add rice and sauté 2 more minutes. Add wine and reduce until almost dry. Add broth, ¼ cup at a time, letting broth reduce until almost gone before adding more. Add cream and fresh herbs. Finish with salt, red pepper, butter and Parmesan. Cool mixture on sheet pan.

Mix in provolone and mozzarella. Form into 2-ounce balls, keeping hands moist with water to prevent sticking. Prepare eggwash by mixing eggs with milk. Roll balls in flour, then in eggwash and bread crumbs. Heat vegetable oil to 350°F and fry rice balls 8 minutes. The oil should be deep enough to cover at least half of balls when frying. Drain on paper towels and serve.

David Brown

Chef David Brown attended Boston University, School of Fine & Applied Arts. He started his culinary career as an intern in the pasty department at the Hyatt Regency in Dallas. His next job took him west to Hawaii, where he was the Executive Pastry Chef at the Hyatt Regency (now Hilton Waikoloa Village) on Hawaii's Big Island. Chef Brown's amazing creations earned him a spot on the 1993 U.S. World Pastry Cup Team, where he went on to receive the Medaille d'Honeur in Lyon, France.

cranberry walnut scone

MAKES **12 SERVINGS**

1	cup fresh cranberries
1	cup orange juice
2	cups all-purpose flour
⅓	cup sugar
2	teaspoons baking powder
¼	teaspoon salt
⅓	cup chilled butter, cut into pieces
⅓	cup heavy cream
1	egg
¼	cup walnuts, chopped and toasted
	Egg wash: 1 egg and 1 teaspoon water

Soak cranberries in orange juice overnight. Combine flour, sugar, baking powder and salt. Rub in butter by hand. Mix in cream and egg just until moistened. Drain cranberries and fold into mix. Mixture will be sticky. Lightly flour table. Knead 4 to 5 times. Pat out to ½-inch thickness and cut out 3-inch circles. Brush tops with egg wash and sprinkle with sugar and walnuts. Place on ungreased baking sheet. Bake at 425°F 11 minutes or until golden brown.

pear helena

MAKES **6 SERVINGS**

- 1 quart Pinot Noir wine
- 12 vanilla beans, split and scraped
- 1 pound dried sour cherries
- 2 quarts water
- 4 pounds sugar
- 6 ripe pears
  Sauce Anglaise (recipe follows)
  Hazelnut Cream (recipe follows)
- ½ cup fresh berries
- 6 sprigs fresh mint

Boil wine, vanilla beans, cherries, water and sugar. Reduce heat to simmer. Carefully peel pears and place in simmering liquid; cook until centers are as soft as outsides. (Each batch of pears cooks differently, so it is wise to poach more pears than are needed; slice into extra pears to check for doneness.) Pour mixture into bowl and place in ice bath. When cool, transfer to airtight container. Cover and marinate 3 or 4 days in refrigerator.

To serve, remove pears from marinade and drain on clean towel. Working from bottom, carefully remove core from pear with Parisian scoop. On dessert plate, make puddle of Sauce Anglaise; place pear in center. Put small scoop of Hazelnut Cream next to pear and garnish with fresh berries and sprig of mint.

Sauce Anglaise

- 2 cups half-and-half
- 6 vanilla beans, split and scraped
- 4 ounces granulated sugar
- 4 egg yolks

Scald half-and-half with vanilla; whip granulated sugar with egg yolks. Temper hot cream into egg mixture, return to heat and cook, constantly stirring until cream thickens. Strain and cool in ice bath.

Hazelnut Cream

- ½ cup whole hazelnuts
- ½ cup powdered sugar
- ½ teaspoon vanilla extract
- 1 cup heavy whipping cream

Roast hazelnuts at 350°F until golden brown. If skins are still on when they come out of oven, rub them between your hands and a clean kitchen towel to remove. Process warm hazelnuts, powdered sugar and vanilla in food processor until nuts are very fine. Whip cream until soft peaks form. Fold in ground nut mixture and refrigerate.

Note: The chocolate swan neck in the photo above was made in a custom mold designed by David Brown. To make your own, roll out plain cookie dough ¼ inch thick. Cut out the shape of a swan head and neck, fill with melted chocolate and chill. After removing the swan, you can touch up edges with a warm butter knife.

Josh Brown

Born in the San Francisco Bay area, Chef Josh Brown fell in love with everything culinary at the age of thirteen. After he graduated from the Santa Barbara City College Culinary Program, he poured himself into his passion and began working at Bouchon in Santa Barbara. One of the highlights of his culinary career was working with Julia Child at a charity cooking event.

whole-head butter lettuce salad

with toasted pine nuts, prosciutto and shaved parmesan with lemon vinaigrette

MAKES **1 LARGE SALAD FOR 1 SERVING**

- 5   ounces prosciutto, cut into thin strips
- 2   tablespoons olive oil
- 2   tablespoons pine nuts
- 1   head butter lettuce
- 2   ounces Parmesan cheese, shaved
    Lemon Vinaigrette (recipe follows)

Preheat oven to 350°F. Fry prosciutto in hot olive oil until crisp; set aside. Sprinkle salt and pine nuts onto a baking sheet and toast in oven 5 minutes; set aside.

Cut with an "X" into top of lettuce. Sprinkle toasted pine nuts and crispy prosciutto into middle of salad; also sprinkle small amount around outer leaves. Drizzle Lemon Vinaigrette all over salad. With a vegetable peeler, shave thin slivers of Parmesan onto top of salad as finishing touch. Serve whole with dinner fork and steak knife.

Lemon Vinaigrette
- 2   cloves garlic, minced
- 1   shallot, minced
- 3   lemons, juiced and zested
- ½   cup olive oil
- 3   tablespoons sweet vinegar (sherry or champagne vinegar)
    Salt and pepper, to taste

Combine garlic, shallot, lemon juice and zest in large mixing or salad bowl. Slowly whisk in olive oil and vinegar. Season with salt and pepper and set aside.

santa barbara ridgeback shrimp and butter lettuce wraps
with roasted tomato vinaigrette

MAKES **4 SERVINGS**

1 pound ridgeback shrimp, cleaned
2 carrots, chopped
2 stalks celery, chopped
1 white onion, diced
2 plum tomatoes, diced
1 tablespoon black peppercorns
2 sprigs fresh thyme
2 bay leaves
2 lemons, juiced
2 Haas avocados, cubed
¼ cup Preserved Lemon Zest (recipe follows)
¼ cup chopped fresh cilantro
 Roasted Tomato Vinaigrette (recipe follows)
2 heads butter lettuce

Poach ridgeback shrimp in large pot with carrots, celery, white onion, tomatoes, peppercorns, thyme and bay leaves approximately 4 minutes. Be careful not to overcook shrimp. Remove from pot and place in ice bath. Once cool, halve shrimp and toss in large bowl with avocado, Preserved Lemon Zest and cilantro and season to taste. Let sit 10 minutes before assembling salad.

To serve, place Roasted Tomato Vinaigrette in dipping bowl; place bowl on large serving platter. Place shrimp mixture in bowl on platter. Arrange lettuce leaves around bowls. Guests roll or wrap shrimp mixture in lettuce leaves and dip in vinaigrette.

Preserved Lemon Zest

5 lemons, zested
¼ cup sugar
¼ cup water
3 sprigs fresh thyme
2 cloves garlic, crushed

Combine sugar and water in small saucepan. Slowly let sugar dissolve over medium-low heat. Add lemon zest, thyme and garlic; simmer about 7 minutes. Remove from heat and allow to cool.

Roasted Tomato Vinaigrette:

4 vine-ripened tomatoes
3 cloves garlic, minced
1 shallot, minced
1 cup olive oil, divided
¼ cup sweet vinegar
1 teaspoon sugar
1 lemon, juiced
 Salt and pepper, to taste

Preheat oven to 350°F. Roast tomatoes, garlic and shallot with ¼ cup olive oil in covered pan 15 minutes. Remove and cool. Once cool, place all of above ingredients in blender; add vinegar, sugar and lemon juice. While blending, drizzle in ¾ cup olive oil and season to taste. Can be made and refrigerated up to 2 days in advance.

Sharon Campbell

Executive Pastry Chef Sharon Campbell graduated from the Culinary Institute of America in Hyde Park, New York, with high honors and the Vatel Club Award. She has taught classes at the Highland Gourmet Cooking School, working with Jacques Pepin, Martha Stewart, and Julia Child. Chef Campbell has worked for the Monterey Plaza Hotel & Spa, where she created 100 to 150 wedding cakes a year. She has appeared on numerous television cooking shows, demonstrating her wonderful pastries.

pumpkin roulade

MAKES **8 SERVINGS**

6	eggs
1	cup sugar
1⅓	cups pumpkin purée
1	tablespoon lemon juice
1	cup sifted all-purpose flour
2	teaspoons baking powder
1	teaspoon ground nutmeg
1	tablespoon ground cinnamon
2	teaspoons ground ginger
½	teaspoon salt
	Caramel Mascarpone Butterscotch Mousse (recipe follows)
	Powdered sugar

Preheat oven to 350°F. Line sheet pan with parchment paper and spray with nonstick cooking spray. Beat eggs and sugar until light and fluffy. Add pumpkin purée and lemon juice; blend until smooth. Fold in remaining dry ingredients. Spread in prepared sheet pan and bake 15 minutes or until center of cake springs back. Cool.

Lay parchment paper on counter. Dust with powdered sugar. Invert roulade sheet onto paper. Spread Caramel Mascarpone Butterscotch Mousse evenly onto roulade. Roll like a burrito and chill. Slice to serve.

Caramel Mascarpone Butterscotch Mousse

¾	cup sugar
2	cups heavy cream, divided
8	ounces mascarpone cheese
¼	cup butterscotch liqueur
1	cup caramel sauce

Caramelize sugar and add 1 cup heavy cream. Cook until smooth; chill. When cool, whip together with remaining ingredients.

pumpkin crème brûlée

MAKES 8 SERVINGS

- 5 cups heavy cream
- 1 vanilla bean, split
- ¾ cup sugar, plus extra for topping
- ½ teaspoon salt
- 15 egg yolks
- 2½ cups fresh puréed pumpkin
- ½ teaspoon ground cinnamon
- ½ teaspoon ground ginger
- 8 mini pumpkins, tops cut off and hollowed out to hold approximately 1 cup filling
  Pumpkin Seed Brown Sugar Tuile Cookie

Preheat oven to 300°F. Bring cream, vanilla, sugar and salt to a boil. Blend egg yolks in small bowl. Add 1 cup hot cream mixture to yolks and whip until blended. Return egg yolk mixture to pot and blend well with puréed pumpkin, cinnamon and ginger. Strain through sieve. Place hollowed pumpkins on greased cookie sheet and fill with crème brûlée mix. Bake approximately 40 to 45 minutes. Custard will be done when set except for quarter-sized circle that will still jiggle. Cool and chill until ready to serve. Sprinkle top of custard with sugar and heat with culinary torch to caramelize sugar. Garnish with Pumpkin Seed Brown Sugar Tuile Cookie.

Pumpkin Seed Brown Sugar Tuile Cookie

- 1 cup brown sugar
- ⅔ cup light corn syrup
- ½ cup cake flour
- ½ cup plus 2 teaspoons all-purpose flour
- 1¼ sticks unsalted butter, melted
- ½ cup pumpkin seeds, toasted

Preheat oven to 300°F. Blend brown sugar, corn syrup, cake flour, all-purpose flour and butter until very smooth. Fold in pumpkin seeds; chill. When dough is cold, scoop into small balls and place on parchment paper. Bake until brown. Let cool before carefully lifting tuile circle off pan. Insert into crème brûlée immediately after caramelizing sugar; hold in place until sugar cools and sets cookie in place.

Marco Cavuoto

Chef Marco Cavuoto is the Executive Chef at Rulli's Restaurant in San Francisco, California.

Laura says...

For a nuttier taste and texture add toasted pine nuts. You will love it!

grape tomatoes and bocconcini

MAKES **4 SERVINGS**

½   pound grape tomatoes
1   bunch fresh arugula
10   kalamata olives, pitted
½   pound mozzarella bocconcini
    (or buffalo mozzarella cut into small pieces)
2   tablespoons balsamic vinegar
½   cup olive oil
5   fresh basil leaves, chopped*
2   fresh oregano sprigs
    Salt and pepper, to taste
    Belgian endive leaves, for
    decoration (2 per plate)

Cut grape tomatoes in half. Finely chop arugula and place in martini glass so it covers bottom of glass. Gently mix together cut tomatoes, olives, bocconcini mozzarella, balsamic vinegar, olive oil, chopped basil, oregano leaves, salt and pepper. Put mixture in glass and garnish with Belgian endive.

Note: An easy way to chop herbs with larger leaves, like basil, is to snip them with clean, sharp kitchen shears.

Chai Chaowasaree

Executive Chef Chai Chaowasaree brought his first restaurant, Singha Thai Cuisine, from Bangkok to Hawaii back in 1988. Singha was chosen as the only Thai restaurant in Hawaii to be certified by the Royal Thai Government. In 1999, Chef Chai opened his second restaurant, Chai's Island Bistro, in Honolulu. He has won numerous awards and has had the pleasure of serving his cuisine to royals from around the world.

blackened fresh ahi summer rolls
with soy ginger sesame sauce

MAKES **4 SERVINGS**

Cajun-style seasoning
4 pieces (3 ounces each) fresh ahi tuna, each about 10 inches long
4 pieces Thai rice paper, each about 12 inches wide
   Radish sprouts and enoki mushrooms
1 ounce shredded carrots
1 ounce shredded cooked beets
1 ounce shredded green mango
16 mint leaves
4 ounces baby lettuce
   Soy Ginger Sesame Sauce (recipe follows)

Sprinkle Cajun seasoning on fish evenly. Quickly sear fish about 30 seconds in hot, nonstick pan; put aside. Soften each piece of Thai rice paper by spraying it with water or covering it with damp cloth. (It will take about 30 seconds to soften.) Lay on flat surface. Divide all ingredients to be wrapped into 4 portions. First, put radish sprouts and enoki mushrooms on end of each paper. Next, layer carrots, beets, green mango, 4 mint leaves, 1 piece ahi and baby lettuce into even layers. Fold rice paper in on each end like a burrito. Continue to roll rice paper into a tube with all ingredients wrapped inside. Repeat this process 4 times. Cut each roll into bite-size pieces. Serve with Soy Ginger Sesame Sauce.

Soy Ginger Sesame Sauce

¼   cup low-sodium soy sauce, or less (to taste)

¼   cup mirin (Japanese sweet rice wine)

½   cup water

1   ounce fresh ginger, sliced

1   ounce onions, sliced

1   ounce celery, sliced

1   ounce carrot, sliced

    Dash sesame oil

2   tablespoons unsalted butter

Place all ingredients except butter in large saucepan. Bring to a boil, then reduce heat and simmer 20 to 30 minutes. Strain vegetables just before serving. Slowly whip butter into remaining sauce. Turn off heat.

Tip: Butter should be at room temperature. When adding butter to sauce, whip continuously until butter is incorporated into sauce. Turn off heat right away.

Fred Clabaugh

Chef Fred Clabaugh has more than 20 years of experience in high-intensity culinary production and fine dining. His early career included positions at The Swan Restaurant in Colorado, the Dining Rooms for the Fairmont Hotels in San Jose and Denver, and Le Profil Restaurant in Denver. He is currently the Executive Chef at the Tenaya Lodge at Yosemite National Park, where he serves his signature "Sierra Alpine Cuisine."

pan-seared california halibut

with white peach tarragon salsa

MAKES **2 SERVINGS**

8 white peaches
4 tablespoons minced fresh tarragon leaves
6 limes, juiced
2 tablespoons cracked peppercorns
2 tablespoons olive oil or butter
2 halibut fillets, 6 ounces each
1 shallot, minced
   All-purpose flour, for dredging
   Salt and pepper, to taste

Cut peaches in half and remove pits. Slice halves into segments and place in medium bowl. Add tarragon leaves, lime juice and cracked peppercorns. Lightly toss together and set aside.

Heat oil or butter in medium frying pan. Season fish with salt and pepper. Add shallots to pan. Sauté until tender. Dredge fish in flour and place in pan with shallots. Cook 2 minutes per side or to desired doneness. Plate fish and pour salsa over top.

Angelo Corvino

Chef Angelo Corvino is the Corporate Chef for Monterey Mushrooms Company. Previously, Chef Corvino worked in the kitchens of The Cypress Room, The Lodge at Pebble Beach, Shadowbrook Restaurant and Amelio's in San Francisco.

Laura says...

Salt draws moisture out of mushrooms, so take care not to over salt mushrooms when using them as an ingredient in a recipe.

sun-dried tomato, mushroom and chicken linguine

MAKES **4 SERVINGS**

4	ounces boneless chicken thighs, cut into pieces
4	to 6 ounces all-purpose flour
3	ounces white mushrooms, sliced
2	teaspoons minced garlic
2	ounces sun-dried tomatoes, julienned
1½	teaspoons sage, rubbed
3	tablespoons brandy
1	cup chicken stock
2	tablespoons butter
3	ounces fresh or parboiled linguine
¼	cup (1 to 2 ounces) grated Parmesan cheese
	Salt and pepper, to taste

Dust chicken pieces with flour.

Sauté chicken with mushrooms, garlic, sun-dried tomatoes and sage.

Deglaze with brandy.

Add chicken stock and cook 2 minutes.

Finish with butter.

Drop pasta in salted boiling water and cook until it floats.

Drain pasta and toss with chicken and sauce. Plate and top with Parmesan. Season to taste.

grilled portabella salad

MAKES 4 SERVINGS

Whisk together extra-virgin olive oil and balsamic vinegar. Add garlic, eggplant, olives and basil. Season with salt and pepper. Toss with spinach. Season again with salt and pepper, if desired.

Mound greens in center of platter. Lay mushroom slices across top of greens. Distribute Gorgonzola cheese over mushrooms. Garnish with roasted tomatoes and Italian parsley.

Seasoning Blend

2½ tablespoons paprika
 2 tablespoons salt
 2 tablespoons garlic powder
 1 tablespoon black pepper
 1 tablespoon onion powder
 1 tablespoon ground red pepper
 1 tablespoon dried oregano
 1 tablespoon dried thyme

Combine all ingredients thoroughly and store in an airtight container. Makes ⅔ cup.

 4 large portabella mushrooms
 2 tablespoons olive oil
    Seasoning Blend (recipe follows)
1½ cups extra-virgin olive oil
 ½ cup balsamic vinegar
 2 teaspoons minced garlic
 ⅔ cup diced grilled eggplant
 ½ cup chopped Italian olives
 2 tablespoons finely chopped basil leaves
 8 cups fresh spinach, cleaned and
      steamed
 1 cup crumbled Gorgonzola cheese
 4 plum tomatoes, split in half and roasted
 1 tablespoon chopped fresh Italian parsley
    Salt and pepper, to taste

Preheat grill. Season portabella mushrooms with olive oil and Seasoning Blend. Place on hot grill and cook 3 to 4 minutes on each side. Remove from grill and slice on the bias.

potato and oyster napoleons

MAKES **4 SERVINGS**

3   **tablespoons unsalted butter**
12   **ounces oyster mushrooms**
½   **cup sliced shallots**
½   **teaspoon salt**
¼   **teaspoon black pepper**
½   **cup chicken stock**
½   **cup heavy cream**
2   **teaspoons chopped fresh thyme**
2   **tablespoons truffle oil**
     Potato Crisps (recipe follows)
½   **cup (about 2 ounces) finely grated Asiago cheese**
12   **slices fresh black or white truffle**
     Fresh arugula tossed with extra-virgin olive oil

Potato Crisps

3   **cups olive oil**
2   **large baking potatoes (such as russets), sliced ⅛ inch thick**
     Whole fresh Italian parsley leaves
½   **teaspoon salt**

Preheat oven to 400°F. Brush 2 large baking sheets with olive oil. Arrange potato slices in 1 layer on sheets. Place whole Italian parsley leaf on each potato slice and top with another slice of potato. Brush with remaining oil. Bake until golden, 12 to 15 minutes, switching sheets halfway through baking. Transfer to cooling rack.

Melt butter over medium-high heat in large heavy skillet. Add mushrooms, shallots, salt and pepper and sauté until soft and most of mushroom liquid has evaporated, about 8 minutes. Add chicken stock, cream and thyme and simmer until liquid has reduced by half in volume, about 5 minutes. Remove from heat and stir in truffle oil. Place 2 potato crisps on each serving plate. Spoon 1 generous tablespoon of mushroom filling on each plate and sprinkle each with 1 teaspoon grated Asiago.

Continue layering Napoleon to a total of 3 layers of potatoes and 3 layers of mushrooms, ending with mushrooms on top. Garnish top of each Napoleon with 3 truffle slices and sprinkle with Asiago. Arrange arugula around outer edge of plate and serve.

James Corwel

Executive Chef James Corwel is one of fewer than 60 Certified Master Chefs (C.M.C.) in the United States. He began his culinary career at the age of 13 and sought out Certified Master Chefs to apprentice under to expand his culinary knowledge. He has worked for Tavolo (a web-based food and wine organization) and later joined the teaching faculty of The Culinary Institute of America at Greystone.

brick-roasted chicken
with apples

MAKES **4 SERVINGS**

2 tablespoons olive oil
1 whole chicken, back removed, wing tips cut off
4 to 5 sprigs fresh thyme
4 to 5 fresh sage leaves
Large brick, wrapped in foil
2 cups button mushrooms
1 cup apples, cut into matchsticks
¼ cup brandy
¼ cup chicken stock
2 to 3 tablespoons cream
½ yellow onion, sliced
1 tablespoon chopped fresh sage
1 tablespoon chopped fresh thyme
Salt and pepper, to taste
Additional fresh herbs (optional)

Preheat oven to 350°F. Add oil to ovenproof skillet, making sure pan is hot before adding chicken. Liberally season both sides of chicken with salt and pepper and place in pan, skin side down. Place thyme and sage on chicken and firmly place foil-wrapped brick on top. Sauté 3 to 5 minutes or until light brown crust is formed. Place pan in oven and cook 35 to 45 minutes. Chicken is done when juices run clear.

Remove chicken gently from pan and set aside, keeping juices and any solids in pan. Discard aromatics or save for garnish. Add mushrooms and apples to pan and sauté 2 to 3 minutes. Add brandy and cook 1 more minute to cook off alcohol. Add chicken stock. Reduce slightly 2 to 3 minutes; add cream to thicken to desired consistency. Season with salt and pepper.

Pour apple and mushroom mixture onto serving platter. Cut chicken into desired portions and place on top. Garnish with fresh herbs.

shaved apple and avocado salad
with candied walnuts

MAKES **4 SERVINGS**

½ cup walnuts
Olive oil, divided
Ground chili pepper
1 tablespoon truffle honey
1 romaine lettuce heart, torn into pieces
Balsamic vinegar
2 cups spinach, chopped
1 apple, julienned
1 pear, julienned
1 avocado, cut into quarters and then sliced
Red wine vinegar
Saba*
Truffle oil
Salt and pepper, to taste

Note: Saba (also called "musto cotto") is a vinegar produced from grape must, a liquid by-product of winemaking. Saba is available in specialty markets or may be ordered from sources on-line.

Toss walnuts in sauté pan with olive oil, salt, chili pepper and truffle honey until coated; set aside to cool.

Mix lettuce and spinach with olive oil, balsamic vinegar, salt and pepper.

Plate lettuce mixture; toss apple and pear in remaining dressing in bowl. Place on top of lettuce. Place avocado on top of each plate and dress with candied walnuts. Drizzle with red wine vinegar, saba and truffle oil before serving.

Eric Ernest & Larry Greenwood

Chef Eric Ernest is the Executive Chef at Royale Restaurant in the Wilshire Royale Hotel, Los Angeles.

Chef Larry Greenwood is the chef at the restaurant in the The Standard Hotel in Hollywood.

Laura says...

A one-pound lobster should take about 10 minutes to cook; cook 3 minutes longer for each additional pound.

maine lobster
with avocado, cherry tomatoes, kaffir lime and young cilantro

MAKES **4 SERVINGS**

4	Maine lobster tails, cooked and cooled
2	cups cherry tomatoes, halved
2	cups avocado, diced
1	kaffir lime, juiced with pulp
1	teaspoon fleur de sel
	Pinch cracked white peppercorn
3	tablespoons extra-virgin olive oil
6	sprigs fresh young cilantro (optional)
	Basil oil (optional)

De-shell lobster tails and slice thin.

Mix lobster meat with tomatoes, avocado, kaffir lime pulp, fleur de sel, white pepper and olive oil in large bowl.

To serve, place small amount of salad on plate or place salad back in lobster shell. Garnish plate or shell with basil oil and young cilantro.

BOA steakhouse signature bone-in rib-eye steak

MAKES **1 SERVING**

1 **(20-ounce) bone-in rib-eye steak**
  Olive oil
  Salt and pepper, to taste
¼ **cup roasted garlic, minced**
  Juice of ½ lemon
2 **tablespoons olive oil**
½ **cup crushed avocado**

Place steak on grill; add salt, pepper and olive oil while it cooks for flavor. Grill evenly on each side 12 to 16 minutes, depending on how you like your meat cooked. Combine garlic, lemon juice, olive oil and crushed avocado and mix thoroughly. Serve with cooked steak.

hand-cut ahi tuna tartare
with avocado, yuzu, mustard oil & black radish

MAKES **4 SERVINGS**

½   cup BOA Steakhouse Cooked Beets
      (recipe follows)

8   ounces ahi tuna, diced, divided

1   tablespoon fleur de sel sea salt

1   teaspoon cracked tellicherry
      peppercorns

1   avocado, quartered and cut into fans

2   tablespoons yuzu juice

2   tablespoons Mustard Oil (recipe follows)

½   cup black radish, julienned

Place 2 tablespoons BOA Steakhouse Cooked Beets in small ring mold in center of plate. Top with 2 ounces tuna. Top with fleur de sel and peppercorns.

Remove mold and place avocado fan on top. Lightly sprinkle avocado with yuzu juice and Mustard Oil, letting excess garnish plate. Sprinkle with black radish. Repeat with remaining ingredients

BOA Steakhouse Cooked Beets

4   whole beets (not peeled)

1   cup mirin (Japanese sweet rice wine)

2   cups water
      Pinch sugar and salt

Mix beets, mirin, water, sugar and salt and bring to a boil. Add beets and simmer 35 minutes. Drain beets from solution, reserving juice and setting beets aside to cool. Place reserved beet juice back on stove over low heat and reduce until liquid has consistency of syrup (about 15 to 20 minutes). Peel and dice cooked, cooled beets. Pour beet reduction over beets.

Mustard Oil
You can buy prepared mustard oil or make your own using this recipe.

1   cup olive oil

2   cups canola oil

2   tablespoons mustard seed

Heat 9-inch skillet over medium-high heat and add canola and olive oil blend. Bring up temperature to about 350°F and add whole mustard seed. Remove from heat and let seeds steep in hot oil about 1 hour. Strain seeds from oil.

Bunyan Fortune

Chef Bunyan Fortune is the Executive Chef at the La Playa Hotel Terrace Grill Restaurant in Carmel.

wonton taco salad

MAKES **4 TO 6 SERVINGS**

8   ounces ground beef
2   cups canned salsa fresca, divided
2   cups Cheddar cheese, divided
2   cups Monterey Jack cheese, divided
1   to 2 packages egg roll or wonton skins
    Vegetable oil, for frying
4   cups romaine lettuce
    Corn tortilla chips or strips

Brown ground beef. Add 1 cup salsa and cook until dry; chill. Add ½ cup each Cheddar and Monterey Jack cheese. Fold mixture in wonton skins and fry in hot vegetable oil. While cooking, toss romaine with remaining salsa and divide evenly among plates. Garnish with remaining cheese, salsa and corn tortilla chips. Arrange wontons decoratively on platter.

provincial california meatloaf

MAKES **6 TO 10 SERVINGS**

½ pound bacon (or pancetta), diced
2 large onions, diced
1 tablespoon minced garlic
8 ounces mushrooms, sliced
1 pint apples, peeled, cored and diced
1 tablespoon kosher salt
2 pounds ground beef
2 large eggs
8 ounces crumbled blue cheese
1 cup bread crumbs
¼ cup chopped fresh parsley
2 tablespoons chopped fresh thyme
1 tablespoon chopped fresh rosemary
1 tablespoon Asiago cheese

Brown bacon and remove from pan. Sauté onions in bacon drippings and add garlic. Remove onions and garlic from pan. Sauté mushrooms and set aside to cool. Sauté apples and set aside to cool.

Once cooled, incorpoate all extra ingredients with chilled ingredients and meatloaf. Form meatloaf or place in pan. Cook at 350°F 20 to 30 minutes. Reduce temperature to 220°F and cook until internal temperature is 160°F. Remove from oven and let stand 10 minutes before serving.

Trey Foshee

Executive Chef Trey Foshee, born in Hawaii and raised in Ojai, California, began working in restaurants because he was a natural around food. He graduated from the New York Culinary Institute of America at 19 and worked at L'Orangerie in Los Angeles, La Folie in San Francisco, and the Bay Terrace in Hawaii. He was named one of "America's Ten Best New Chefs" by Food and Wine Magazine in 1998 and was offered a job as Executive Chef and co-owner at George's at the Cove in La Jolla, California.

seared rare albacore
with ligurian black olive smashed potatoes and shaved young artichoke salad

MAKES **4 SERVINGS**

4   pieces (5 ounces each) albacore tuna
1   tablespoon olive oil
    Salt and white pepper
    Smashed Potatoes (recipe follows)
    Artichoke Salad (recipe follows)

Heat pan over high heat. Add olive oil. Season tuna with salt and pepper and sear on all sides, keeping rare on inside. Slice into ½-inch slices. Divide Smashed Potatoes among 4 plates and top with sliced tuna. Place Artichoke Salad on side.

Smashed Potatoes
1   Yukon Gold potato, peeled
¼   cup Ligurian black olives, pitted and minced
2   tablespoons chopped fresh Italian parsley
8   tablespoons extra-virgin olive oil
    Salt and freshly ground white pepper, to taste

Place potatoes in medium pot and cover with cold water. Season generously with salt and cook over medium heat until potatoes are tender. You can hold them 45 minutes at this point over low heat. When ready to serve, remove potatoes with slotted spoon and place in mixing bowl. Smash potatoes with fork until no large lumps remain. Add olives, parsley, olive oil and a little potato cooking liquid. Mix well and season with salt and white pepper.

Artichoke Salad
4   fresh young artichokes
2   tablespoons Meyer lemon juice
3   tablespoons extra-virgin olive oil
½   cup arugula sprouts

Break off outer leaves of artichokes until you get to inner, tender leaves. Trim tops of artichokes. Using a paring knife or vegetable peeler trim off any green at artichokes' base and rub each artichoke with sliced lemon to prevent discoloration. Slice artichokes paper thin into medium bowl. Add lemon juice, olive oil and sprouts and toss to combine.

Andrew Gibson

Chef Andrew Gibson is the chef de cuisine for Bacara Resort & Spa in Santa Barbara, California. Many of his daily dishes include herbs and fruits grown in the property's ten-acre organic gardens. Chef Gibson, who studied at the Culinary Institute of America in Hyde Park, New York, and worked under Todd Humphries at the Wine Spectator Greystone Restaurant, believes that it's important to always begin with quality organic ingredients.

spinach tofu salad
with spicy miso dressing

MAKES **4 SERVINGS**

¼ cup rice wine vinegar
1 tablespoon soy sauce
2 tablespoons yellow miso
1 tablespoon sambal
½ tablespoon sugar
2 tablespoons chopped pickled ginger
1 teaspoon sesame oil
½ cup canola oil
1 pound firm tofu, cut lengthwise into slices
1 bag (6 ounces) baby spinach
½ cup chopped green onions
1 tablespoon toasted sesame seeds
   Freshly ground white pepper, to taste

Combine rice wine vinegar, soy sauce, miso, sambal, sugar and chopped pickled ginger in a blender; blend until smooth. With mixer running, drizzle in sesame and canola oils to form an emulsion. Place in large bowl. Brush tofu slices with dressing. Place baby spinach in bowl and toss with remaining dressing. Add green onions.

Place 1 piece tofu on center of plate. Add some baby spinach. Add another piece tofu and more spinach. Continue this process until you are out of tofu. Drizzle with dressing left in bottom of bowl and garnish with toasted sesame seeds. Season with white pepper, if deisred.

miso soup
with tofu and spinach

MAKES **4 SERVINGS**

2   cups water
4   tablespoons miso paste
8   to 10 ounces soft tofu, diced
1   bag (6 ounces) baby spinach, chopped
2   green onions, sliced thin

Bring water to a boil. Dissolve miso completely in water; add tofu, baby spinach and green onions. When almost at a boil, remove from heat and serve.

baked tofu
with wilted spinach and peanut sauce

MAKES **4 SERVINGS**

⅓   cup unsalted shelled peanuts
3   tablespoons soy sauce
1½ teaspoons sugar
¼   cup water
2   tablespoons canola oil
½   ounce fresh ginger, minced
2   cloves garlic, minced
3   green onions, white parts only, minced
1   pound baked tofu, diced
1   bag (6 ounces) baby spinach

Pulverize peanuts in blender. Add soy sauce, sugar and water, and mix on low. When thoroughly mixed, sauce will look like runny peanut butter. Heat oil in large skillet; add ginger, garlic, green onions, tofu and baby spinach. Cook until spinach is wilted; strain away any liquid.

To plate, place baby spinach and tofu mixture in center of plate and drizzle peanut dressing around.

Hervé Glin

Chef Hervé Glin's love of seafood and many of his culinary ideas come from his native France, but his experience at some of the best restaurants in Washington, DC, Napa Valley, and Houston have added an American accent to his cooking. He has created menus and opened restaurants all over California.

scrambled eggs
on smoked salmon and russet potato napoleon with chive cream

MAKES **1 SERVING**

1 large russet potato, finely sliced lengthwise (you will need 3 chips per person)
　Vegetable oil, for frying
2 large eggs, beaten
　Freshly ground pepper, to taste
2 ounces smoked salmon
⅓ cup chopped chives, divided
½ cup sour cream
1 tablespoon capers
½ red onion, sliced

Fry potato chips in oil heated to 375°F (look for chips to turn golden and become crispy). When cooked, remove chips from oil and place on paper towels to drain any excess oil. Scramble eggs softly with freshly ground pepper. Julienne smoked salmon (cut into long, fine strips). Add half of chives to sour cream.

To construct napoleon, place a touch of sour cream in middle of plate and place first chip on it. Cover chip with 2 tablespoons scrambled eggs, 1 tablespoon of sour cream mix and one-fourth of smoked salmon. Repeat same operation 1 more time and layer third chip on top. Finish with drop of sour cream and chives. Place capers and chives around napoleon, with slices of red onion for garnish.

poached eggs
on russet potato pancake
with smoked chipotle pork

MAKES **1 SERVING**

1   **large potato, cooked (toss potato with salt and olive oil and wrap in aluminum foil; bake)**

½   **cup ground pork sausage, cooked with 1 teaspoon chopped chipotle**

½   **cup chopped green onions**

½   **cup sour cream**

3   **eggs, divided**

2   **tablespoons butter**

    All-purpose flour

½   **cup white vinegar**

    Salt and freshly ground pepper, to taste

    Cherry tomatoes and chives

The day before, remove insides of cooked potato and smash with fork (should be about 1½ cups). Add cooked pork sausage, green onions, sour cream and 1 beaten egg. Mold mixture into 3-inch circle (1 inch tall) using piece of PVC pipe or something with similar tube shape. Cool overnight.

The day of, heat 8-inch nonstick skillet with 2 tablespoons butter. Coat potato pancake with flour. Cook pancake on both sides until golden. Meanwhile, poach 2 large eggs in boiling salted water with white vinegar (1 quart water and ½ cup vinegar). Run eggs under warm water to remove excess vinegar. Place pancake on plate; top with 2 eggs. Season with salt and pepper; garnish with cherry tomatoes and chives.

grilled pork tenderloin on wild mushroom potato risotto
with chipotle honey drops

MAKES **4 SERVINGS**

2 pork tenderloins
Chopped fresh thyme leaves
Kosher salt
Cracked black pepper
Wild Mushroom Potato Risotto (recipe follows)
Chipotle Honey Drops (recipe follows)

Preheat grill to medium-high heat. Season pork as desired with thyme, salt and pepper flakes.

Grill pork to desired doneness. Slice thinly across the grain. Serve with Wild Mushroom Potato Risotto and garnish as desired with Chipotle Honer Drops.

Wild Mushroom Potato Risotto
¼ cup butter
⅓ cup chopped shallots
1 tablespoon fresh thyme leaves
1 pound portobello, shiitake or chanterelle mushrooms, diced
1½ pounds red or Yukon Gold potatoes, finely diced

½ cup white wine
1 cup chicken stock
1 cup heavy cream
½ cup grated Parmesan cheese
Salt and white pepper, to taste

Melt butter in saucepan with shallots, thyme and mushrooms until mushrooms are soft. Add diced potatoes and white wine. Reduce by half. Add chicken stock and cream. Bring to a boil and cook 2 minutes. Add Parmesan cheese. Season with salt and white pepper.

Chipotle Honey Drops
¼ chipotle pepper in adobo sauce
½ cup honey
2 tablespoons white vinegar
1 cup ketchup

Blend all ingredients together and keep chilled.

Carlos Guia

Chef Carlos Guia grew up in Venezuela, where he helped his New Orleans-born mother cook. Classically trained in French-style cuisine, Chef Guia also incorporates his Venezuelan culture and New Orleans' roots into his cooking. He cooked at Le Bernardin in New York and in Commander's Palace in New Orleans before moving to Las Vegas to helm the kitchen of the Commander's Palace in the Planet Hollywood Hotel.

strawberry shortcake
with sweet buttermilk biscuits

MAKES **8 SERVINGS**

4	cups all-purpose flour
½	teaspoon kosher salt
1½	tablespoons baking powder
3½	cups granulated sugar, divided
1	cup (2 sticks) cold butter, cut into 1-inch cubes
1½	cups buttermilk
1	teaspoon baking soda
4	pints strawberries*
1½	cups very cold heavy cream
¼	cup granulated sugar
	Powdered sugar (optional)

Smaller strawberries are generally sweeter. If using smaller berries, use less sugar.

Preheat oven to 400°F. Sift flour, salt, baking powder and ½ cup sugar in large bowl. Gently work in butter using 2 forks or hands, breaking butter into pea-size pieces but taking care not to overwork dough.

Mix buttermilk with baking soda. Make a well in center of dry ingredients, pour buttermilk mixture into well. Gently combine to moisten dry ingredients. Lightly fold just until sticky, wet dough forms. (The less dough is handled, the flakier the biscuits will be.)

Lightly dust work surface with flour. Gently flatten dough into 1½-inch-thick disk. Cut into 8 biscuits with flour-dusted 2½-inch round cutter. Set biscuits touching each other in ungreased baking sheet. Bake biscuits 20 to 25 minutes. Do not overbake; biscuits continue to cook as they cool.

Wash and hull strawberries. Cut in half vertically; if they are large, cut into quarters. One hour before serving, combine berries and up to 3 cups sugar (to taste). Set aside 1 hour. Berries and sugar will produce syrupy liquid as they sit.

Prepare whipped cream just before serving. Whip chilled heavy cream in chilled bowl with whisk or electric mixer. Add sugar when cream starts to thicken; whip to desired consistency. (Do not overbeat.)

To serve, split the still-warm biscuits horizontally and dust top halves with powdered sugar. Place bottom halves of biscuits on dessert plates and top each with portion of strawberry mixture and some of their syrup. Top with whipped cream and sugared biscuit tops.

creole seasoned and grilled pork tenderloin

with oven-dried strawberry-port wine reduction and goat cheese stone-ground grits

MAKES **8 SERVINGS**

1 tablespoon butter

½ cup sliced shallots

1 tablespoon chopped garlic

4 sprigs fresh thyme

2 bay leaves

4 cups oven-dried strawberries,* divided

2 cups port wine

2 cups veal stock

4 pounds fresh pork tenderloin, trimmed of fat and silver skin

4 tablespoons Creole seasoning

Olive oil

Kosher salt and freshly ground black pepper, to taste

Goat Cheese Stone-Ground Grits (recipe follows)

You may purchase sun-dried or dried strawberries, or you can make your own by simply tossing halved or quartered strawberries with sugar (1 cup strawberries to 1 tablespoon sugar). Place on nonstick pan skin down and cook at 150°F approximately 3 hours. Remove from oven and cool. Strawberries should shrink but still be moist. Refrigerate in airtight container.

Heat heavy 2-quart saucepan over medium heat. Add butter and shallots; caramelize. Add garlic, thyme, bay leaves, half of oven-dried strawberries and pinch salt and pepper. Cook 2 minutes over low heat and deglaze with port wine. Reduce port by half, add veal stock and keep reducing until nape (sauce will coat back of wooden spoon). Adjust seasoning to taste and strain through fine mesh strainer. Add remaining oven-dried strawberries and keep hot.

Preheat grill 30 minutes. Season pork tenderloins with creole seasoning and some light olive oil. Grill pork, rotating to mark all sides. Lower grill temperature or finish in 350°F oven until pork's internal teperature reaches 140°F (medium preparation). Remove from heat and allow to rest 5 minutes. Slice pork and arrange on platter with Goat Cheese Stone-Ground Grits and Oven-Dried Strawberry-Port Reduction.

Goat Cheese Stone-Ground Grits

2 cups water

4 ounces stone-ground grits

3 ounces goat cheese

½ cup whole milk

½ tablespoon fresh thyme leaves

Salt and pepper, to taste

To cook grits, bring water to a boil. Add grits and reduce heat to simmer. Simmer 5 minutes, remove from heat and cover about 30 minutes, adding more hot water, if necessary. When ready to serve, add whole milk, goat cheese, thyme, salt and pepper.

pan-seared foie gras
with strawberry-black pepper gastrique and savory pistachio bread pudding

MAKES **8 SERVINGS**

1 (1½-pound) Grade A foie gras
2½ cups fresh strawberries, divided
2 cups white balsamic vinegar
2 cups light corn syrup
1½ teaspoons black pepper, cracked, divided
 Kosher salt, to taste
 Pistachio Bread Pudding (recipe follows)

Pistachio Bread Pudding
2 loaves French bread (8 inches long)
2 large eggs
1¼ cups milk
1 cup chopped pistachios, divided
¼ teaspoon salt
½ teaspoon white pepper, ground
4 tablespoons unsalted butter

Keep foie gras at room temperature 30 minutes. Heat large pot of water and place long, thin-bladed knife into it. Once blade is hot, slice foie gras into 8 equal portions, each weighing about 3 ounces. If slices are thick, gently pound with flat mallet to ½- to ¾-inch thickness and refrigerate.

Make gastrique by mixing balsamic vinegar, corn syrup, 2 cups sliced strawberries and 1 teaspoon cracked black pepper in 2-quart saucepan. Reduce by half and strain with fine mesh strainer; keep warm. Dice remaining strawberries and add to gastrique with remaining black pepper. Consistency should be syrupy but not too thick. Once foie gras has chilled completely, season with kosher salt and sear in dry skillet over medium to high heat. Cook until browned (only about 30 seconds); flip and repeat. Serve with Pistachio Bread Pudding and Strawberry-Black Pepper Gastrique.

Quarter bread and slice into ½-inch slices. In large bowl whisk together eggs, milk, salt and pepper. Add bread to egg mixture and massage until bread is soaked. Refrigerate at least 2 hours, stirring occasionally. Lightly toast ½ cup pistachios and mix into pudding.

Butter 8-inch cake pan or other baking dish and coat all sides with ½ cup of raw pistachios. Pack bread pudding mix pan. Sprinkle top with remaining pistachios; push lightly so they sink halfway into bread pudding. Double-wrap with foil and bake at 250°F 15 to 25 minutes. Pudding is done when toothpick inserted into center is clean and dry when removed. Remove from oven and refrigerate until cool.

Heat bottom of pan over low flame and loosen sides with knife. Invert onto cutting board. Cut bread pudding into 8 wedges. Rub butter on bottom and sides and reheat in a 250°F oven 10 minutes or until hot throughout.

Jonathan Hale and Thomas Francque

After Executive Chef Jonathan Hale studied at the Culinary Institute of America he moved to Hawaii where he developed a love for fresh fruits, vegetables, and seafood. He moved back to the mainland and took up residence in San Diego where his passion for fresh ingredients continues.

Thomas Francque is the chef at Marché Cafe in the Fifth Street Public Market in Eugene, Oregon.

balsamic-marinated sweet onions
with french green beans, prosciutto and tomatoes

MAKES **2 SERVINGS**

1   sweet onion, thinly sliced
1   cup balsamic vinegar, preferably aged, at least enough to cover onions
1   pound French green beans, blanched
2   ounces garlic, chopped
1   red tomato, sliced
8   ounces prosciutto, thinly sliced

Combine onions and balsamic vinegar; set aside at least 2 hours. Cook French beans in salted boiling water 1 to 2 minutes or until crisp. Remove and place in ice bath. Combine garlic, tomatoes, French beans and onions in bowl. Season with salt and pepper. Top with prosciutto.

french onion soup

MAKES **4 SERVINGS**

4	sweet onions
	Olive oil
1	pound sweet onions, chopped small
2	ounces butter
2	ounces brandy
1	quart beef broth
2	bay leaves
	Small sprigs fresh thyme and fresh rosemary
	Salt and pepper, to taste
4	French bread croutons
8	ounces Gruyère cheese

Preheat oven to 350°F. Make onion bowls by peeling onions and scooping out middle. Reserve remaining onion for soup. Place onion bowls on pan. Coat with olive oil, salt and pepper. Cook in oven until soft and lightly browned, approximately 20 minutes.

Dice remaining onions and sauté in large pan with butter until golden brown. Cook gently over low heat to completely caramelize onion, 20 to 30 minutes. Add water if needed to prevent burning.

Deglaze pan with brandy. Add beef broth, bay leaves and herb sprigs. Simmer until onions are tender, approximately 30 minutes. Adjust seasoning with salt and pepper. Remove herbs. Place soup in onion bowls. Top with croutons and shredded Gruyère cheese. Melt in oven until golden brown.

onion rings in beer batter
with garlic aioli

MAKES **2 SERVINGS**

1 tablespoon yeast
3 tablespoons vegetable oil
1 bottle (12 ounces) beer (lager or ale)
2 tablespoons all-purpose flour, or more
   to taste
   Canola oil, for frying
2 large sweet onions
   Garlic Aioli (recipe follows)

Blend yeast, vegetable oil, beer and flour in medium bowl. Set mixture out at warm or room temperature about 2 hours.

Heat oil to 375°F in large pot. Stir batter until smooth again (stir in additional flour if thicker batter is preferred).Slice onions into rings. Coat onion rings in batter and carefully add to hot oil. Cook 3 to 4 minutes or until golden brown. Remove onion rings with slotted spoon and drain on paper towels. Serve with Garlic Aioli.

Garlic Aioli
12 cloves garlic
 2 cups mayonnaise
 2 ounces chives, chopped
    Salt and pepper, to taste

Preheat oven to 300°F. Roast garlic in olive oil until soft. Remove from oven and cover with foil. When cool, mash into a paste with remaining ingredients.

Karen Hatfield

Chef Karen Hatfield began her culinary career in Southern California and continued her way across the country to New York City. While in New York, she worked at many award-winning restaurants, such as Gramercy Tavern, Jojo, and Vong. She then moved to San Francisco, where she worked at Cortez Restaurant. Returning to her hometown of Los Angeles, she opened Hatfield's with her husband, Quinn.

crème fraîche vanilla panna cotta
with bing cherry compote

MAKES 6 TO 8 SERVINGS

1	quart cream
4	ounces sugar
1	vanilla bean
	Pinch freshly grated nutmeg
3½	sheets bloomed gelatin
1	cup crème fraiche
	Cherry Compote (recipe follows)

Bring cream, sugar, vanilla and nutmeg to a boil. Stir in gelatin and crème fraîche and pass through fine mesh sieve; cool. Pour into prepared molds. Refrigerate until set, approximately 3 hours.

To serve, dip mold in hot water and unmold into bowl. Spoon Cherry Compote around panna cotta.

Cherry Compote

1	quart sweet cherries, pitted
¼	cup sugar
½	cup water
¼	cup ruby port
½	cup raspberry purée

Preheat oven to 350°F. Combine all ingredients and roast in oven 15 to 25 minutes.

sour cherry sangria

MAKES 6 TO 8 SERVINGS

1	pound sour cherries, washed and pitted
1	cup lemon juice
1	cup super-fine sugar
1½	cups white rum
1½	cups white wine
1	cup sparkling water (add just before serving)
	Fresh mint, for garnish

Combine all ingredients and pour over ice.

cherry, apricot and almond spiced crumble

MAKES 6 TO 8 SERVINGS

¾	cup almonds, lightly toasted
2	cups all-purpose flour
¾	cup dark brown sugar
1	cup plus 2 tablsepoons granulated sugar, divided
¼	teaspoon ground cinnamon
¼	teaspoon ground ginger
6½	ounces butter
½	teaspoon vanilla extract
2	quarts cherries, pitted and halved
1	quart apricots, pitted and diced large
1	cup sugar

Combine almonds, flour, brown sugar, 2 tablespoons granulated sugar, cinnamon and ginger in bowl. Mix in butter and vanilla with electric mixer on low speed; continue to mix until only very small pieces of butter remain. Spread out on sheet tray and let dry slightly at room temperature; refrigerate until needed.

Stir together cherries, apricots and remaining 1 cup sugar. Cover and refrigerate at least 2 hours.

Pour fruit filling into 4-quart baking dish. Top with refrigerated crumble topping. Bake at 325°F until fruit is bubbling and topping is golden.

KAREN HATFIELD | 55

Bob Hurley

Chef Bob Hurley began cooking professionally more than 25 years ago, first as a chef at the award-winning Domaine Chandon and later as Executive Chef at the Napa Valley Grille. After many years, he opened his own restaurant, Hurley's Restaurant, in Yountville—the epicenter of Napa Valley. He has always had a strong belief that the use of regional, seasonal ingredients is, on many different levels, important to the success of the restaurant.

grilled pork chops
with rosemary roasted potatoes and cherry relish

MAKES **8 SERVINGS**

6	cups water
3	tablespoons salt
2½	tablespoons sugar
1	teaspoon dry thyme
1	bay leaf
6	pork chops (8 ounces each)
	Olive oil
	Chopped fresh thyme and fresh parsley
	Cherry Relish (recipe follows)
	Roasted potatoes

Combine water, salt, sugar, thyme and bay leaf; immerse pork 6 hours. Remove pork, pat dry and marinate by brushing meat liberally with olive oil, thyme and parsley. Let sit 30 minutes to 1 hour.

Season pork with salt and pepper. Grill over low to moderate heat until lightly pink in center. Spoon cherry relish on top. Serve with roasted potatoes.

Cherry Relish

1	tablespoon butter
½	yellow onion, diced
1	teaspoon diced jalapeño pepper
1	teaspoon finely chopped ginger
	Zest of 1 orange
¾	cup sugar
½	cup cherry juice
1	cup raspberry vinegar
½	teaspoon ground cumin
1	teaspoon ground coriander
2	cups fresh cherries, pitted and halved

Melt butter in medium skillet. Add chopped onion and cook until soft. Add remaining ingredients except cherries and bring to a boil. When boiling, add cherries. Toss and reduce by half. Lay out on sheet pan or platter to cool. Serve at room temperature.

valhrona chocolate almond torte
with cherry compote

MAKES **4 SERVINGS**

5 ounces butter
6½ ounces almond paste
2½ ounces sugar
3 large eggs, beaten
2 ounces cocoa powder
4½ ounces chopped chocolate pieces
  Cherry Compote (recipe follows)
  Whipped Cream (optional)
  Toasted Almonds (optional)

Preheat oven to 350°F. Using beater attachment on hand mixer, beat butter until soft and fluffy. Slowly add almond paste until thoroughly mixed. Add sugar. Once thoroughly incorporated, slowly add beaten eggs; on low speed add cocoa powder. Fold in chocolate pieces and cherries by hand.

Divide among 4 (5-ounce) baking cups, and bake 20 minutes. Let cool before removing from cups.

Serve with Cherry Compote, garnished with whipped cream and toasted almonds.

Cherry Compote

1 tablespoon sweet butter
1 tablespoon light brown sugar
½ cup cherry juice
1 pound pitted cherries
  Lemon zest
  Squeeze of lemon juice

Melt butter. Add brown sugar while stirring; add cherry juice and reduce heat by half. Add cherries and cook until soft. Add lemon zest and juice to adjust acid.

John Jackson

Chef John Jackson grew up in a small town where fresh food was a focus. His recipes always follow a simple course, "let your ingredients do the talking." Chef Jackson is the Executive Chef at Vitrine Restaurant in the St. Regis Hotel, San Francisco.

Laura says...

Nectarines can be substituted for either peaches or apricots in most recipes.

nectarine soup

MAKES **2 SERVINGS**

6 eggs
6 nectarines
  Olive oil
  Pepper, to taste
1 cup sugar
1 cup water
  Raspberry Coulis (recipe follows)

Cut nectarines in half and remove pits. Cut each nectarine half into 4 pieces.

Bring sugar and water to boil (375°F). Reduce heat to simmer and cook 5 to 7 minutes. Add sliced nectarines, remove from heat and purée to soup consistency. Strain into airtight container; cool completely in refrigerator. Serve cold, garnished with Raspberry Coulis.

Raspberry Coulis
1 cup sugar
1 cup water
2 pints raspberries

Bring sugar and water to boil. Turn down to a simmer. Let simmer 5 to 7 minutes. Remove from heat and cool.

Combine raspberries and cooled syrup in blender. Purée, and then strain into airtight container.

pan-seared scallop plum risotto

MAKES **5 SERVINGS**

10 scallops
1 stick butter
2 tablespoons vegetable oil
4 large shallots
1 box risotto rice
2 cups plum wine
2 cups plum juice
½ pound plums, diced
4 tablespoons mascarpone cheese
Salt and pepper, to taste

Salt and pepper tops and bottom of scallops. In large pan add scallops, 1 tablespoon butter and oil; sauté over high heat. Sear scallops on 1 side until golden brown; turn over. Reduce heat to low. Remove from heat after 4 minutes or medium rare.

Cook shallots in thick-bottomed pot until they become iridescent. Add risotto rice and cook until toasted. Add plum wine and cook until odor of alcohol has dissipated. Add plum juice and cook, stirring continuously, until rice is al dente (soft on outside harder on inside). Remove from pot and place on pan lined with wax paper. Cool in refrigerator.

Melt remaining butter in thick-bottomed pot. Add risotto and stir with wooden spoon until heated. Fold in plums and mascarpone cheese. Salt and pepper to taste.

Laurence Jackson

Chef Laurence Jackson is the former Executive Chef of Jordan's Restaurant in the Claremont Hotel & Spa in San Francisco.

Laura says...

It takes about 250 cherries to make one cherry pie, so one cherry tree can produce enough cherries for 28 pies!

pork fillet
with sweet and sour cherry sauce and mashed potatoes with green peas

MAKES **4 SERVINGS**

4 (4-ounce) pork fillets
1 cup Sweet and Sour Cherry Sauce (recipe follows)
4 cups mashed potatoes
4 cups green peas, cooked

Grill pork fillets 8 or 9 minutes on each side. You may also cook these pork fillets in pan on stove. Brown all sides; place in 400°F oven 8 to 10 minutes or until desired doneness. Serve with Sweet and Sour Cherry Sauce alongside mashed potatoes and green peas.

Sweet and Sour Cherry Sauce
3 teaspoons lime juice
2 teaspoons sugar
½ teaspoon garlic chili sauce
2 teaspoons green onion, chopped
1 teaspoon chopped fresh cilantro
1 cup fresh cherries
2 teaspoons pineapple juice
¼ cup white wine vinegar

Combine all ingredients in saucepan over medium heat. Reduce 20 to 25 minutes, stirring occasionally, until mixture has a sauce consistency.

cinnamon chili crusted pork ribs
with BBQ cherry sauce, baked baby potatoes and cole slaw

MAKES **4 SERVINGS**

1 tablespoon ground cinnamon
1 tablespoon chili powder
1 tablespoon ancho chili powder
1 tablespoon chipotle chili powder
1 teaspoon curry powder
3 pounds pork ribs
1 cup BBQ Cherry Sauce (recipe follows)
½ pound baby potatoes, baked until soft
6 cups Cole Slaw (recipe follows)

Mix cinnamon, chili powders and curry powder; rub over ribs and season with salt and pepper. Grill ribs about 12 minutes on each side or until done. Serve with BBQ Cherry Sauce, baked baby potatoes and Cole Slaw.

BBQ Cherry Sauce

1 onion, chopped
1 tablespoon olive oil
1 cup white wine
½ cup white wine vinegar
2 teaspoons Worcestershire sauce
2 tablespoons sugar
1 cup fresh cherries
Zest of 1 lemon
Salt and pepper, to taste

Sauté onion in olive oil in medium skillet until translucent. Add all other ingredients. Cook over medium heat until it reduces by half (about 20 minutes).

Cole Slaw

1 pound cabbage, sliced
¼ pound red cabbage, sliced
2 carrots, julienned
⅓ cup champagne vinegar
½ cup mayonnaise
1 teaspoon sugar
½ cup pineapple juice
Salt and pepper, to taste

Mix vinegar, mayonnaise, sugar, pineapple juice, salt and pepper together until smooth. Toss cabbage and carrots with mayonnaise mixture. Serve as side dish.

Jeffrey Jake

Chef Jeffery Jake is the Executive Chef of The Carneros Inn in Napa Valley, where he incorporates fresh local ingredients into his cooking. As a native of Napa, he began his career as a sous chef at Domaine Chandon in Yountville and also served as chef de cuisine at Pebble Beach, Beach and Tennis Club; Sonoma Mission Inn; and The Old Bath House Restaurant. Chef Jake has conducted cooking courses at the Culinary Center of Monterey and has taught California cuisine cooking classes in Japan.

alsatian green onion tart

MAKES **4 SERVINGS**

3   bunches green onions
1   cup vegetable broth
2   tablespoons heavy cream
1   cup chopped crisply cooked bacon
4   (5-inch) puff pastry rounds
3   tablespoons olive oil
3   tablespoons red wine vinegar
3   tablespoons minced fresh chervil
    Salt and pepper, to taste

Slice white parts only of green onions; reserve green tops for later use. Combine sliced onions with broth in a saucepan over low heat. Cook until onions are soft, about 15 minutes; drain and transfer to bowl to cool. When cool, stir in heavy cream and bacon. Season with salt and pepper.

Julienne reserved green onion tops; mix with olive oil, red wine vinegar and chervil. Season with salt and pepper.

Place 2 puff pastry rounds on each of 2 parchment paper-lined baking sheets. Prick pastry all over with fork to reduce rising. Divide onion and bacon mixture among pastry rounds and spread to cover pastry. Bake in preheated 350°F oven 15 to 20 minutes or until pastry is golden brown. Cool slightly and then top with marinated onion salad.

potato-garlic dip with capers
with fennel pita toasts and mixed green salad

MAKES **8 SERVINGS**

Potato-Garlic Dip

- 2 cups day-old bread
- 3 to 5 garlic cloves
- ⅓ cup extra-virgin olive oil
- ¼ cup capers, preferably salt packed, rinsed and drained, divided
- 3 to 4 tablespoons lemon juice, freshly squeezed, divided
- ½ cup blanched whole almonds, soaked overnight in water and drained
- 1 medium potato, peeled, boiled and mashed

    Salt and freshly ground white pepper, to taste

    Mixed Green Salad (recipe follows)

    Fennel Pita Toasts (recipe follows)

Soak bread in water just until soft. Squeeze excess water out. Process bread and garlic in food processor until smooth paste forms. With motor running, gradually add oil. Add 3 tablespoons capers and 3 tablespoons lemon juice. Add almonds; pulse until coarsely ground. Transfer to medium bowl.

Fold in mashed potato. Season to taste with salt, white pepper and lemon juice. Cover and refrigerate at least 2 hours.

Arrange Mixed Green Salad on individual serving plates. Top with dip and serve with Fennel Pita Toasts.

Mixed Green Salad

- 2 tablespoons olive oil, or more to taste
- 2 tablespoons lemon juice, or more to taste

    Salt and pepper, to taste

- 1 bag (7 ounces) mixed greens

Whisk together oil, lemon juice and salt and pepper. Add greens and toss to coat.

Fennel Pita Toasts

- 4 loaves pita bread, cut into eighths
    Olive oil
    Fennel seeds

Preheat oven to 350°F. Arrange pita triangles on baking sheet and brush with olive oil. Sprinkle with fennel seeds or other seasoning and bake until edges become crisp. Transfer to wire rack and cool completely.

monterey bay salmon paillards
with central coast mixed greens, artichokes and sweet tomatoes drizzled with artichoke-lemon and olive oil emulsion

MAKES **4 SERVINGS**

Salmon Paillards

- 4 salmon fillets (4 ounces each), skins removed
- 2 tablespoons olive oil
- 1 teaspoon chopped fresh thyme
- 4 teaspoons unsalted butter
  Salt and white pepper, to taste
  Mixed Green Salad (recipe follows)
- 4 cups mixed greens
- 8 currant or cherry tomatoes, halved
- ¼ cup feta cheese (optional)
  Sautéed Baby Artichokes (recipe follows)
  Artichoke-Lemon and Olive Oil Emulsion (recipe follows)

Place salmon fillets between 2 sheets plastic wrap sprinkled with water to prevent sticking. Gently pound fillets with mallet while drawing mallet toward you to form ¼-inch-thick paillards. Combine olive oil and thyme; pour over salmon paillards and marinate.

Melt butter in nonstick skillet. As butter begins to brown, place salmon in skillet and season with salt and pepper. Cook over medium heat 2 minutes as butter continues to brown. Turn fillets and continue to cook another 30 to 40 seconds. Remove fish from skillet.

Toss mixed greens, tomatoes, feta cheese and Sautéed Baby Artichokes with Artichoke-Lemon and Olive Oil Emulsion. Season with salt and pepper and arrange on serving platter. Top with salmon fillets.

Sautéed Baby Artichokes

- ½ cup olive oil
- 1 tablespoon butter
- 1 green onion, chopped
- 1 garlic clove, chopped
- 1 carrot, finely diced
- 8 baby artichokes, cut in half and placed in acidulated water
- ⅓ cup dry white wine
- ¼ cup water
  Salt and pepper, to taste

Heat large skillet over medium-high heat. Add olive oil, butter, green onion, garlic and carrots. Sauté 2 minutes, and then add drained and dried artichokes. Season with salt and pepper. Cook 2 minutes. Add white wine and water to skillet. Reduce heat and simmer 5 minutes or until artichokes are tender. Remove artichokes from liquid and allow to cool completely; then refrigerate until needed. Continue cooking liquid until reduced to ½ cup; strain and reserve for emulsion.

Artichoke-Lemon and Olive Oil Emulsion

- ½ cup reserved artichoke cooking liquid
- 2 tablespoons fresh lemon juice
- 1 cup olive oil
- 1 teaspoon chopped fresh dill, chopped
  Salt and pepper, to taste

Place cooking liquid and lemon juice in non-reactive bowl. Slowly whisk in olive oil and dill. Season with salt and pepper.

Wally Joe

Wally Joe is chef and co-owner of KC's Restaurant, a Cleveland, Mississippi restaurant started by his Hong Kong-born parents more than 30 years ago. He has hosted many James Beard dinners. His unique cooking style features his family's native cuisine alongside down-home Southern fare.

cauliflower couscous

MAKES 4 SERVINGS

1	head cauliflower, cored and cut into 1½-inch chunks
¼	cup prepared Italian salad dressing
¼	teaspoon salt
⅛	teaspoon ground black pepper

Pulse cauliflower in food processor just until size of cooked couscous. Do not purée. In 12-inch nonstick skillet, heat salad dressing over medium heat; cook cauliflower, stirring frequently, until crisp-tender, about 10 minutes. Stir in salt and pepper and serve immediately.

citrus italian pork tri-tip
with tomato salad

MAKES **4 SERVINGS**

¾ cup prepared Italian garlic marinade, divided

1 orange, sectioned (reserve 2 tablespoons juice)

1 pork tri-tip (1½ to 2 pounds)

2 medium red and/or yellow tomatoes, cut into thin wedges

2 tablespoons chopped red onion

2 tablespoons Italian dressing

2 tablespoons fresh parsley or basil, chopped

Salt, to taste

Pour ½ cup Italian marinade blended with reserved orange juice over pork in large, shallow, non-aluminum baking dish or plastic bag. Cover, or close bag, and marinate in refrigerator 30 minutes.

Meanwhile, combine tomatoes, orange sections, onion, dressing, parsley or basil and salt; set aside.

Remove pork from marinade, discarding leftover marinade. Grill or broil pork, turning once and brushing frequently with remaining ¼ cup Italian marinade, until pork reaches desired doneness. Serve topped with tomato salad.

"fauxtato" soup

MAKES **4 SERVINGS**

2   cups water
1   packet dry mushroom soup mix
1   bag (20 ounces) frozen cauliflower
1   jar (16 ounces) Alfredo sauce
    Crumbled bacon (optional)
    Shredded Cheddar cheese (optional)
    Chopped green onion (optional)

Combine water, mushroom soup mix, and cauliflower in 3-quart saucepan. Bring to a boil over high heat. Reduce heat to medium-low and simmer, covered, 5 minutes or until cauliflower is tender.

Purée soup in batches in food processor or blender until smooth. Return soup to saucepan and stir in Alfredo sauce. Simmer over medium-low heat 3 minutes or until heated through.

Garnish with crumbled bacon, shredded Cheddar cheese, and chopped green onion.

orange shrimp and fennel salad

MAKES **4 SERVINGS**

1   **cup olive oil vinaigrette dressing**
1   **tablespoon grated orange peel**
2   **teaspoon chopped fresh rosemary**
1   **pound uncooked medium shrimp, peeled and deveined**
1   **medium head fennel, trimmed and cut into ¼-inch wedges**
8   **cups baby spinach**
1   **orange, peeled and sectioned**

Make marinade by combining dressing, orange peel and rosemary in small bowl. In large, non-aluminum baking dish or plastic bag, pour ¼ cup marinade over shrimp and fennel. Cover, or close bag, and marinate in refrigerator 30 minutes. Refrigerate remaining marinade.

Remove shrimp and fennel, discarding used marinade. Grill or broil shrimp and fennel, turning once, brushing occasionally with ¼ cup reserved marinade. Cook 4 minutes or until shrimp turn pink and fennel is tender. To serve, arrange spinach on serving platter, and then top with hot shrimp and fennel. Garnish with orange slices and drizzle with remaining ½ cup reserved marinade.

David Paul Johnson

Chef David Paul Johnson's early jobs as a dishwasher at a pizza parlor and positions at The Rodeway Inn and IHOP led him to his career in the culinary world. Chef Johnson has worked in the kitchens at the Hyatt Regency Waikiki, Hawaii and in his own restaurant and catering company. He has also cooked in some of the most award-winning kitchens in the world, including Charlie Trotter's in Chicago, Aujourd'Hui in Boston, and Bistro de l'Etoille in Paris.

grilled "steak and eggs" odon buri style
with maui onion jus

MAKES **4 SERVINGS**

1	cup premium Japanese cooking rice
1	cup purified water
½	tablespoon unsalted butter
1	teaspoon finely chopped, peeled fresh ginger
2	tablespoons cooking oil, divided
4	(4-ounce) ground beef patties
	Salt and pepper, to taste
1	cup Maui onions, thinly sliced
1	tablespoon tamari soy sauce
2	cups beef stock
2	ounces red wine
2	ounces port wine
2	tablespoons cooked rice
	Salt and pepper, to taste
4	quail eggs

Wash rice; drain thoroughly. Pour purified water over rice in small saucepan fitted with lid and let rest 30 minutes. Uncover; place over medium-low heat, add butter and ginger and bring to a slow boil. Reduce heat to simmer and cover. Continue cooking an additional 10 minutes or until all liquid has been absorbed. Remove lid to air out rice. Using flat spatula, gently turn rice and leave it uncovered 5 minutes. Replace lid and keep warm until serving.

Heat flat-bottomed cast iron skillet until it just starts to smoke over medium-high heat. Reduce heat to low add 1 tablespoon oil. Season beef patties with salt and pepper and place in pan. Cook about 2 minutes per side (for rare) or to desired doneness. Remove from pan and keep warm.

In the same skillet, increase heat to medium-high and pour off any remaining drippings from patties. Once pan starts to smoke again, add remaining cooking oil and sliced onions. Cook until caramelized, stirring occasionally and allowing them to brown but not burn. When onions are an even brown color, add soy sauce and cook until reduced. Add stock, red wine, port and rice; increase heat to medium-high. Bring

to a boil, and then reduce heat to medium and continue cooking until liquid is reduced by half. Pour into blender and blend until smooth. Return to skillet and continue cooking over low heat; season to taste. Sauce should be slightly thickened and have a slight shine.

To assemble, place one-fourth of cooked rice in shallow bowl. Place cooked meat on top, grill or pan fry quail egg "sunny side up" and place on top of patty. Spoon sauce around these ingredients and serve.

Jean-Marie Josselin

Chef Jean-Marie Josselin is from the French Alps region of France and was educated at Paris' Mederic Culinary School. After working his way through the top restaurants and hotels of Europe and the United States, he arrived in Hawaii in 1988 and opened A Pacific Café. He has won numerous awards and has been a featured chef at the James Beard House.

stir-fried chinese broccoli
with garlic and black beans

MAKES 2 SERVINGS

18	young Chinese broccoli
2	tablespoons sesame oil
2	tablespoons minced fresh garlic
¼	cup minced Chinese fermented black beans
2	tablespoons minced fresh ginger
2	tablespoons oyster sauce
6	Chinese parsley sprigs

Bring large saucepan filled with water to a boil; add salt to taste. Add Chinese broccoli and cook about 30 seconds. Remove from boiling water and place broccoli in water bath with ice cubes. Remove from water and reserve on paper towel. Heat sesame oil in large wok or skillet over high heat. When almost smoking add minced garlic, black beans and ginger. Stir until they release fragrance (about 10 seconds). Add broccoli and sauté until warm, about 2 minutes. Add oyster sauce and chopped Chinese parsley. Stir well and serve immediately.

stir-fried chicken
with yellow curry

MAKES **2 SERVINGS**

3 tablespoons peanut or vegetable oil
2 tablespoons minced fresh ginger
2 tablespoons minced fresh garlic
2 cups diced boneless, skinless chicken
   breast
1 cup diced Japanese eggplant
1 cup diced zucchini
1 cup diced yellow squash
4 kaffir lime leaves
3 tablespoons white wine
½ cup chicken stock
1 cup coconut milk
2 tablespoons yellow curry paste
3 tablespoons diluted corn starch

Heat oil until almost smoking. Add ginger and garlic; stir well to combine until both ingredients are fragrant, about 15 seconds. Add chicken; cook about 5 minutes or until chicken starts to brown. Stir often to avoid burning chicken and having it stick to wok. Add vegetables, combine well and cook an additional 2 minutes. Add kaffir lime leaves and deglaze wok with white wine. Cook 15 seconds to reduce liquid. Add chicken stock, bring to a simmer and add coconut milk. Bring to a simmer. At this point, you can either finish sauce with cornstarch or serve without it.

Norman Kolpas

Norman Kolpas doesn't consider himself a chef, but more a lover of good food, since he has never cooked professionally in a restaurant. He has written more than 30 cookbooks, including such best-sellers as *A Cup of Coffee, Pizza California Style,* and *Gourmet Sandwiches.* In addition, he has worked as consulting editor on the cookbook publishing program created for Williams-Sonoma.

smoky ham-and-cheese beef burgers

MAKES **4 SERVINGS**

1¼ pounds ground beef
¼ pound honey-glazed smoked ham, finely chopped
4 burger buns
2 tablespoons unsalted butter, melted
¼ pound smoked Cheddar cheese, cut into thin slices
2 tablespoons honey mustard (optional)

Preheat grill. Mix ground beef and chopped ham with clean hands in mixing bowl. Form mixture into 4 equal patties about ¾ inch thick; set aside. Wash hands. Brush cut sides of burger buns with melted butter.

Carefully oil grill rack. Grill burgers until done medium-well, 12 to 14 minutes, turning once. About 2 minutes before they are done, place cheese slices on top. Place buns cut sides down on grill; toast just until golden.

Place burgers on toasted buns and, if you like, serve with honey mustard.

Quick tips and variations:

Prepackaged, sliced cooked ham of any kind works well for this recipe.

Feel free to substitute smoked mozzarella cheese or provolone cheese for the Cheddar, or use a good, mild-to-sharp nonsmoked Cheddar.

A honey mustard works well with the flavors in this recipe. If you don't have a jar of honey-flavored mustard, you can make your own by mixing 3 parts Dijon or brown mustard with 1 part honey. Or use another mustard or condiment of your choice.

pizzaiola burgers

MAKES **4 SERVINGS**

2   cloves garlic, peeled and cut into halves, divided
4   fresh basil leaves
1½ pounds ground beef
½   cup Parmesan cheese, grated
2   tablespoons tomato paste
1   tablespoon dried oregano
1   teaspoon sugar
4   soft sandwich rolls or burger buns, split
2   tablespoons extra-virgin olive oil

Preheat grill. Turn on a food processor fitted with metal blades and drop 3 garlic clove halves and basil leaves through feed tube to finely chop. Stop machine, and scrape down sides of work bowl. Add ground beef, Parmesan, tomato paste, oregano and sugar. Pulse machine on and off several times until ingredients are well mixed. With clean hands, form mixture into 4 equal round patties about ¾ inch thick. Set patties aside. Wash hands. Brush cut sides of rolls with olive oil.

Carefully oil grill rack. Grill burgers until done medium-well, 12 to 14 minutes, turning once. During last 2 minutes of cooking, place roll halves oiled sides down on grill; toast until golden.

Quickly rub toasted side of each roll half lightly with cut side of remaining garlic clove half. Place burger on bottom half of each roll and serve with condiments for guests to add to taste.

Quick tips and variations:

Top the burgers with sliced or shredded mozzarella cheese about 2 minutes before they are done.

Shredded fresh basil leaves make a fine addition to the meat mixture.

Sliced sun-ripened tomatoes go very well with these burgers.

Emeril Lagasse

Chef Emeril Lagasse grew up in the small town of Fall River, Massachusetts. He got his start in the restaurant business by learning the art of bread and pastry baking while working at a Portuguese bakery. Chef Lagasse went on to earn a degree from Johnson and Wales University, from which he later was awarded an honorary doctorate degree.

Upon return to the United States, he worked in many of the fine restaurants in New York, Boston, and Philadelphia before heading to New Orleans. He was enticed to New Orleans by Dick and Ella Brennan, who offered him the executive chef position at their award-winning restaurant, Commander's Palace. He accepted, and for seven and a half years showcased his talent and skills there.

In 1990, Chef Lagasse opened the Mobil Travel Guide Four-Star Emeril's Restaurant in the Warehouse District of New Orleans. Now he is the chef-proprietor of nine restaurants, including three in New Orleans (Emeril's, Nola, and Emeril's Delmonico), two in Las Vegas (Emeril's New Orleans Fish House and Delmonico Steakhouse), two in Orlando (Emeril's Orlando and Emeril's Tchoup Chop), one in Atlanta (Emeril's Atlanta), and one in Miami (Emeril's Miami Beach). He has earned numerous awards and recognition, making him extremely popular to food-loving Americans everywhere.

In 1993, Chef Lagasse became a national TV personality — viewers look forward to hearing his signature "BAM" while he creates his dishes. He is also the food correspondent for Good Morning America on Friday mornings. Along with his restaurants, signature products, and television shows, Chef Lagasse is a best-selling author of more than twelve cookbooks. In September 2002, Emeril established the Emeril Lagasse Foundation support and encourage programs creating developmental and educational opportunities for children.

grilled pork chops
with Emeril's™ Sweet Original BAM BBQ Sauce

MAKES **4 SERVINGS**

4   center-cut bone-in pork chops, at least
    ¾ inch thick, trimmed of excess fat
4   teaspoons Emeril's™ Rib Rub, divided
2   tablespoons olive oil, divided
1   cup (or more) Emeril's™ Sweet Original
    Bam B Q Sauce

Preheat grill to medium heat (about 350°F.).

Season each pork chop with 1 teaspoon Emeril's Rib Rub and then brush with olive oil. Place chops on grill and cook 15 to 20 minutes, turning over often. Brush chops with Emeril's™ Sweet Original Bam B Q Sauce each time they are turned. Serve immediately with grilled corn and potato salad.

Recipe Courtesy of Emeril Lagasse, emerils.com

emeril's baby arugula salad
with tomatoes, vidalia onions and popcorn shrimp

MAKES **4 SERVINGS**

1 (5-ounce) package Emeril's™ Baby Arugula
1 cup diced tomatoes
½ cup Vidalia onions, thinly sliced into half rings
½ cup Emeril's™ Romano, Caesar or House Herb Vinaigrette dressing
Salt and cracked black pepper (to taste)
Popcorn Shrimp (recipe follows)

Toss arugula, tomatoes and onions with dressing in large bowl. Season to taste with salt and pepper. Divide among 4 large plates and garnish with Popcorn Shrimp. Serve immediately.

Popcorn Shrimp
2 large eggs beaten
2 tablespoons heavy cream
4 teaspoons Emeril's™ Original Essence, divided
1½ cups plain bread crumbs
6 cups vegetable oil, for frying
1 pound small shrimp, deveined

Whisk together eggs, heavy cream and 2 teaspoons Emeril's™ Original Essence in medium non-reactive bowl. Whisk well to combine. Toss bread crumbs with remaining 2 teaspoons Essence in separate bowl.

Heat oil to 360°F in 1-gallon stockpot over medium-high heat.

Stir one-quarter of shrimp into egg mixture. Soak shrimp in marinade up to 5 minutes. Remove shrimp, shaking off excess egg mixture, Toss with bread crumbs to coat. Place shrimp in coarse sieve and sift excess breadcrumbs into another clean bowl.

Place breaded shrimp into hot oil and fry, stirring occasionally, until golden brown, about 2 minutes. Remove shrimp from hot oil with slotted spoon and drain on paper-lined sheet pan; set aside until needed. Repeat with remaining shrimp. Use immediately after frying last shrimp.

Recipe Courtesy of Emeril Lagasse, emerils.com

Damaso Lee

Damaso Lee, executive chef and owner of Trattoria Acqua Restaurant in La Jolla, California, has spent his entire culinary career in fine-dining Italian restaurants. Chef Lee has completed advanced courses at the prestigious Culinary Institute of America in Napa Valley. He has also been trained in French cooking techniques at the Mobil Travel Guide Five-Star award-winning French Laundry in Yountville, California.

grilled pork tenderloin and stuffed tomatoes
with artichoke hearts, goat cheese and basil

MAKES **6 SERVINGS**

1   (2-pound) boneless pork loin roast
1   jar sweet apricot cooking and grilling sauce, divided
    Stuffed Tomatoes with Artichoke Hearts, Goat Cheese
    and Basil (recipe follows)

Combine pork loin and half of apricot sauce in food storage bag; seal and refrigerate at least 1 hour or up to 36 hours.

Preheat grill to medium-high. Remove pork loin from marinade and place pork loin on grill rack (discard marinade). Cover grill and cook, turning occasionally. Reserve half remaining sauce; occasionally brush pork loin with one half remaining apricot sauce. Grill until pork's internal temperature reaches 160°F to 165°F. Remove from grill, cover and rest 10 minutes before slicing thinly. Heat reserved sauce and pour over sliced pork. Serve with Stuffed Tomatoes.

**Stuffed Tomatoes with Artichoke Hearts,
    Goat Cheese and Basil**
1½   cups artichoke hearts packed in water, chopped
10   fresh basil leaves, julienned
  1   cup crumbled goat cheese
  6   ripe tomatoes
     Bread crumbs
     Salt and pepper, to taste

Preheat oven to 350°F. Mix artichoke hearts with fresh basil and goat cheese. Cut off tops of tomatoes. Remove seeds and stuff with herbed artichoke and cheese mixture. Bake 10 minutes. Sprinkle with bread crumbs, season with salt and pepper and serve.

panzanella tomato salad

MAKES **6 SERVINGS**

6 slices French bread baguette, cut into ½-inch cubes

1 hot house cucumber, cut into ½-inch cubes

½ medium red onion, thinly sliced

4 assorted tomatoes, cut into ½-inch cubes

½ cup kalamata olives

½ cup fresh arugula

   Red Wine Vinaigrette (recipe follows)

   Salt and pepper, to taste

10 fresh basil leaves (optional)

Preheat oven to 375°F. Spread bread cubes on ungreased cookie sheet and bake 5 minutes. Cool. Toss to combine with remaining ingredients except Red Wine Vinaigrette and basil. Drizzle with vinaigrette and toss until evenly coated. Salt and pepper to taste. Garnish with basil leaves.

Red Wine Vinaigrette

¼ cup finely chopped shallots

1 cup red wine vinegar

2 cups olive oil

   Salt and pepper, to taste

Place shallots and vinegar in bowl. Blend with hand blender. With blender running, gradually add olive oil and mix until emulsified. Season with salt and pepper.

gazpacho
chilled tomato soup

MAKES **6 SERVINGS**

2 pounds ripe tomatoes, quartered

2 bell peppers, chopped

½ cup chopped celery

¼ cup chopped fennel bulb

¼ cup chopped red onion

2 tablespoons chopped shallot

2 small garlic cloves, chopped

2 tablespoons champagne vinegar

2 tablespoons extra-virgin olive oil

1 teaspoon fresh thyme

   Salt and pepper, to taste

Blend all ingredients in blender until smooth (if necessary blend in 2 batches, using half of all ingredients in each batch). Force through large sieve into clean bowl. Chill 1 hour. Divide into bowls and serve.

Sandra Lee

Sandra Lee grew up in a small town in Washington State. After her parents divorced and her mom remarried, she became responsible for her younger brothers and sisters. She taught herself how to turn budget-friendly packaged foods into delicious special meals for her siblings.

After attending the University of Wisconsin-LaCrosse, she created her own line of patented home products for do-it-yourself home decorating. Next, she moved into producing gardening products, which were widely distributed in major chain stores. Soon after, she took her products on-air and expanded into crafts, floral, and scrapbooking products.

In 2002, Sandra released her first cookbook, in which in her 70/30 philosophy (70% ready-made products with 30% fresh and creative touches) revealed itself.

Sandra considers herself a lifestyle expert more than a chef since she incorporates easy-to-do tips and techniques for ready-made products. She has appeared on numerous television shows, where she has offered her philosophy on decorating and cooking. With more than twelve book titles to her name, she is also the host of a top-rated television show, Semi-Homemade Cooking. Through her various charities, Sandra is committed to helping others reach for their dreams.

creamy ranch chops and rice

MAKES **4 SERVINGS**

1 tablespoon vegetable oil

4 boneless pork chops, ¾ inch thick

1 can (10¾ ounces) cream of mushroom OR 98% fat free cream of mushroom soup

½ soup can (about 5½ ounces) milk

1 package (1 ounce) ranch salad dressing mix

Paprika

Ranch-Style Rice

Heat oil in skillet. Add chops and cook until browned. Add soup, milk and ½ package salad dressing mix (reserve remaining salad dressing mix for other use). Heat to a boil. Cover and cook over low heat 10 minutes or until done. Sprinkle with paprika. Serve with Ranch-Style Rice.

Tips: To make Ranch-Style Rice add remaining ½ package salad dressing mix to water used to make rice.

dijon glazed pork chops

MAKES **6 SERVINGS**

6 boneless pork chops, ¾ inch thick*
3 tablespoons cornstarch
1 can (14 ounces) chicken broth
2 tablespoons Dijon mustard
6 cups hot cooked rice

Season chops with garlic powder and pepper.
Spray nonstick skillet with vegetable cooking spray.
Heat 1 minute. Add chops and cook until browned.

Mix cornstarch, broth and mustard. Add to skillet.
Cook and stir until mixture boils and thickens.
Cover. Cook over low heat 10 minutes or until done.
Serve with rice.

vegetables
with broccoli lemon sauce

MAKES **8 SERVINGS**

12 smaller red potatoes, cut into quarters

1 large green *or* red pepper, cut into ¼-inch rings

2 cups broccoli florets

1 can cream of broccoli OR 98% fat free cream of broccoli soup

½ cup mayonnaise

4 green onions, finely chopped

1 tablespoons lemon juice

¼ teaspoon dried thyme leaves, crushed

Place potatoes with water to cover in saucepan. Heat to a boil. Cover and cook over low heat 10 minutes. Add pepper and broccoli.

Cook 5 minutes or until vegetables are tender.

In a separate saucepan: Mix soup, mayonnaise, onions, lemon juice, and thyme in saucepan. Heat through. Serve over vegetables.

Louis Lepe

Executive Chef Louis Lepe is a second-generation chef; his father worked at the Zapotlan Country Club in Guadalajara, Mexico. He is a graduate of the Orange Coast College culinary arts program as well as the California School of Culinary Arts Le Cordon Bleu pastry program.

spring salad
with sunflower vinaigrette

MAKES 2 SERVINGS

5   ounces spring mix lettuces
8   apple slices
    Sunflower Vinaigrette (recipe follows)
1½ ounces Caramelized Walnuts (recipe follows)
6   raspberries

Mix lettuces and fold in apple slices. Drizzle with Sunflower Vinaigrette and add Caramelized Walnuts. Garnish with fresh raspberries.

Sunflower Vinaigrette
1   apple, chopped
2   tablespoons sunflower seeds
1   teaspoon brown sugar
1   teaspoon chopped fresh garlic
3   tablespoons apple cider
½   cup olive oil
    Salt and pepper, to taste

Blend chopped apple with sunflower seeds in food processor or blender. Mix with brown sugar. Add garlic, apple cider and olive oil. Season with salt and pepper.

Caramelized Walnuts
½   teaspoon granulated sugar
4   ounces whole walnuts
    Powdered sugar
2   tablespoons vegetable oil

Dissolve granulated sugar in 2 teaspoons water over medium heat. Add nuts. Cover and cook 20 minutes. Remove walnuts, dust with powdered sugar; set aside for 15 minutes. Heat oil in small skillet. Sauté walnuts until sugar caramelizes; spread on sheet pan to cool.

apple turnovers

MAKES **1 SERVING**

1 apple, sliced
1 teaspoon butter
1 ounce brown sugar
1 teaspoon cinnamon
2 tablespoons apple cider
1 egg
¼ cup water
1 piece puff pastry, 2-inch square
3 ounces cream cheese or goat cheese
3 ounces walnuts
  Powdered sugar
  Caramelo Sauce (optional)

Sauté fresh, sliced apple with butter, brown sugar and cinnamon. Deglaze pan with apple cider. Poor mixture into bowl and let cool completely.

Preheat oven to 350°F. Whisk together egg and water. Grease baking sheet or line with parchment paper. On floured surface, roll out puff pastry into 2 equal 2-inch square pieces; place side-by-side on baking sheet. Place about 2 tablespoons apple filling, 3 ounces cream cheese and walnuts in middle of 1 puff pastry piece. Brush edges with egg wash and fold other puff pastry piece over apple filling. Crimp edges with fork tines. Brush top of turnover with egg wash and sprinkle with powdered sugar. Bake 15 minutes or until lightly browned. Serve with vanilla ice cream and Caramelo Sauce, if desired.

Caramelo Sauce

4 tablespoons sugar
1 teaspoon water
1 tablespoon butter

Heat sugar with water. Cook until golden brown. Add butter and melt to finish.

Rudy Liebl

Chef Rudy Liebl pursued a culinary education at the famous La Varenne in Paris and learned about the wines of the world at the Academy Du Vin. He has also trained under the acclaimed chefs James Beard and Marion Cunningham. Chef Liebl has won numerous awards, including being named the California Restaurant Association's 2002 Chef of the Year.

alaskan halibut
with white nectarine and apricot garlic sauce

MAKES **4 SERVINGS**

4	tablespoons oil, divided
3	cloves garlic, chopped
1½	cups apricot nectar
4	fresh mint leaves, chopped
¼	cup chicken stock
	Red pepper flakes, to taste
2	white nectarines, peeled and cut into wedges
4	(8-ounce) halibut fillets
	Salt and white pepper, to taste
	All-purpose flour, to dredge

Heat 2 tablespoons oil in large skillet. Sauté garlic; just before it turns brown, add apricot nectar, mint leaves, chicken stock, red pepper flakes, salt and pepper. Reduce to syrupy consistency. Add nectarine wedges and cook until they are heated through. Set aside.

Dredge halibut in flour; shake off excess. Sauté in heated skillet with remaining oil and cook until desired doneness. Place on plate. Quickly heat nectarine sauce and pour over top of halibut.

atlantic sea scallops
with white nectarine salsa

MAKES **4 SERVINGS**

Scallops

2 cups Japanese bread crumbs (panko)
¼ teaspoon salt
1 teaspoon seafood seasoning
2 eggs
¼ cup cream
½ cup balsamic vinegar
¼ cup honey
12 large sea scallops
¼ cup grape seed oil
½ cup all-purpose flour
   White Nectarine Salsa (recipe follows)
   Enoki mushrooms

White Nectarine Salsa

4 nectarines, peeled and diced
4 tablespoons chopped fresh cilantro
½ medium sweet red onion, diced
¼ teaspoon salt
⅛ teaspoon white pepper
¼ cup olive oil
   Juice of 3 lemons

Combine ingredients and marinate 3 hours.

Combine bread crumbs, salt and seasoning and set aside. Mix eggs and cream and set aside. Combine balsamic vinegar and honey in small saucepan and cook over medium-high heat until reduced to syrupy consistency. Let cool.

Heat grape seed oil in large skillet over low heat. Dredge scallops in flour, shaking off excess. Dip one side of a scallop in egg mixture; then, press same side firmly in Japanese bread crumbs. Place in skillet bread crumb-side down. Cook until golden brown; turn over and finish cooking (approximately 2 minutes). Repeat with all scallops. With slotted spoon, place one-quarter of White Nectarine Salsa on each of 4 plates and top with 3 scallops. Garnish with balsamic vinegar syrup and Enoki mushrooms.

Leslie Mackie

Chef Leslie Mackie developed her culinary skills at the California Culinary Academy in San Francisco. Baking became her true love while she worked at Biba in Boston. After working as a restaurant consultant, she was intrigued by the science of bread making. She began working as head baker at Seattle's Grand Central Bakery. In 1993, she opened her own place, Macrina. She has appeared on Julia Child's "Baking with Julia" TV series and has been nominated "Best Pastry Chef" by the James Beard Foundation.

la dolce gorgonzola
with fresh cherry compote

MAKES 4 SERVINGS

8	ounces Gorgonzola Dolce
2	cups fresh cherries (Bing and Rainier)
1½	tablespoons sugar
1½	tablespoons white wine
¾	cup roasted walnuts
1	teaspoon freshly grated lemon peel
1	teaspoon coarsely chopped fresh oregano
1	(1-pound) rustic baguette
	Kosher salt and freshly cracked black pepper, to taste

Divide Gorgonzola into 4 pieces. Arrange on 4 salad plates. Pit cherries and cut into halves. Place cherries in small skillet and add sugar and white wine. Cook 3 minutes, dissolving sugar warming cherries. Toss cherries with walnuts, lemon peel and oregano. Season with salt and pepper. Spoon compote on plate and serve with 3 slices fresh baguette.

Variation: Brush each slice of baguette with olive oil and toast before serving.

chocolate and brandied cherry tart

MAKES **1 (10-INCH) TART**

5 ounces unsweetened chocolate, coarsely chopped

¾ cup (1½ sticks) unsalted butter, at room temperature

1½ cups granulated sugar

1 tablespoon unbleached all-purpose flour

6 eggs

2 cups Brandied Cherries (recipe follows)

1 baked 10-inch tart shell

Powdered sugar

Lightly sweetened whipped cream

Preheat oven to 300°F. Combine chocolate and butter in medium stainless steel bowl. Place bowl on top of saucepan filled with 2 inches simmering water, making sure that bottom of bowl does not come in contact with water. It is important that water be just simmering; if it is too hot it will scorch ingredients. Stir chocolate and butter with rubber spatula until they are completely melted and combined. Remove bowl from heat and let cool to room temperature.

Whisk together granulated sugar, flour and eggs. Add to bowl of cooled chocolate and mix with rubber spatula until all ingredients are thoroughly combined and mixture has thickened.

Place baked tart shell on rimmed baking sheet. Scatter 1 cup drained Brandied Cherries over bottom of tart shell, and then pour chocolate mixture over cherries, filling shell to just below the top. Place baking sheet on center rack of oven and bake about 30 minutes or until center is just set. Let cool on wire rack 30 minutes. Remove sides of pan and dust tart lightly with powdered sugar. Serve warm with spoonful of remaining Brandied Cherries and garnish with lightly sweetened whipped cream.

Brandied Cherries

½ cup granulated sugar

½ cup brandy

1 tablespoon pure vanilla extract

¼ cup filtered water

2 cups Bing cherries, stemmed and pitted

2 tablespoons unsalted butter (optional)

Combine sugar, brandy, vanilla extract and water in medium saucepan and bring to a simmer over medium heat. Add cherries and stir with wooden spoon to make sure all fruit is coated. Reduce heat to low and cook 3 minutes, stirring frequently. Cover pan and remove from heat. Let cherries steep 1 hour. At this point cherries are ready for use in cake or tart recipes. Store in airtight container in refrigerator up to 1 week.

To make a nice brandied cherry sauce, reheat cherries and stir in 2 tablespoons butter. The sauce is a nice accompaniment to tarts or cakes, spooned over ice cream or on your favorite pancakes.

Michelle Mah

Korean-born Chef Michelle Mah got her start in cooking at her family table. After majoring in Ethnic Studies at the University of California San Diego, Chef Mah went on to the California Culinary Academy for her culinary degree. A master of French-California brasserie cuisine, Chef Mah loves to cook Vietnamese, Chinese, Thai, and Korean dishes.

hot spiced fuji apple cider

MAKES 4 SERVINGS

1 quart fresh Fuji apple cider
1 cinnamon stick
¾ cup apple brandy
¼ cup unsweetened whipped cream

Heat all ingredients until warm. Taste cider; for a sweeter beverage, add 1 tablespoon sugar at a time, to taste.

Garnish each cup with small dollop of whipped cream.

quick apple, almond and pine nut tart

MAKES 8 SERVINGS

8 (4-inch) squares puff pastry
4 Granny Smith or Fuji apples, peeled, cored and sliced very thin
¼ cup granulated sugar, plus extra to dust before baking
½ tablespoon ground cinnamon
  Pinch ground nutmeg
1 tablespoon fresh lemon juice
1 (7-ounce) tube pure almond paste
½ cup pine nuts
½ cup (1 stick) butter, melted
  Powdered sugar and whipped cream (optional)

Preheat oven to 375°F. Place cut puff pastry pieces on baking sheet lined with parchment or waxed paper. Toss sliced apples with granulated sugar, cinnamon, nutmeg and lemon juice and set aside. Spread small amount of almond paste on each puff pastry, using more or less depending on how much you like almond flavor. Sprinkle pine nuts over almond paste. Arrange apples on puff pastry. Brush lightly with melted butter.

Bake 15 to 20 minutes or until golden brown. Dust with powdered sugar and top with whipped cream.

grilled char siu pork chops
with gingered applesauce

MAKES **2 SERVINGS**

½ cup sugar
1 star anise
1 teaspoon ground cinnamon
1 teaspoon ground white pepper
½ teaspoon salt
¼ cup Chinese rice wine or dry vermouth
1 tablespoon dark soy sauce
1 tablespoon soy sauce
1 tablespoon tomato paste
2 (12-ounce) center-cut pork chops

Bring all ingredients except pork to a simmer and stir periodically until all sugar has melted; simmer about 10 minutes so all spices infuse together.

Cool marinade completely before pouring half over pork chops. Marinate overnight or at least 8 to 10 hours. Reserve other half of marinade.

Grill pork until medium, about 10 to 12 minutes total, basting with reserved marinade.

Gingered Applesauce
3 Granny Smith or Fuji apples, peeled, cored and chopped into chunks
⅓ cup sugar
½ cup riesling wine or pineapple juice
1 (1-inch) piece fresh ginger, peeled and julienned
3 star anise
1 (2-inch) cinnamon stick
Juice of 1 lemon

Cook all ingredients in 2-quart saucepan over medium heat 15 to 20 minutes or until apples have broken down.

Robert Mancuso

Certified Executive Chef Robert Mancuso of Sardine Factory in Monterey, California, graduated from the Culinary Institute of America in Hyde Park, New York, with high honors. He is the recipient of numerous national and international culinary awards and was a member of the 1996 Culinary Olympic Team USA. Chef Mancuso has pursued international studies and participated in culinary competitions in Brazil, England, and Germany, winning 13 gold medals.

chilled seafood ceviche

MAKES **4 TO 6 SERVINGS**

1	pound fresh red snapper fillets
⅓	cup lime juice
¼	cup orange juice
1½	cups diced red onion, divided
¼	cup diced celery
2	tablespoons diced green bell pepper
2	tablespoons diced red bell pepper
2	tablespoons diced yellow bell pepper
½	cup peeled, seeded and diced tomatoes
¼	cup sliced green onions
1	teaspoon red pepper flakes
1	teaspoon salt
¼	cup tomato juice
1	cup diced avocado
¼	cup chopped fresh cilantro
6	sprigs fresh cilantro
18	lime wedges
18	Croutons (recipe follows)

Cut snapper into ½- to 1-inch cubes. Mix with juices, ½ cup diced red onion, celery, peppers, tomatoes, green onions, chili flakes and salt. Marinate in refrigerator 4 hours, stirring every hour; fish should take on an opaque appearance. After 4 hours, add tomato juice and let marinate 1 more hour. Fold in diced avocado and chopped cilantro. Serve chilled on decorative platter garnished with remaining red onion, cilantro sprigs, lime wedges and Croutons.

Croutons

1	(1-pound) loaf baguette bread
½	cup olive oil or clarified butter
1	teaspoon salt

Preheat oven to 325°F. Slice baguette on the bias, ¼ inch thick. Lightly spray or brush slices on both sides with oil or clarified butter. Sprinkle with salt. Place slices on baking sheet and toast 8 to 10 minutes or until golden brown.

Video instructions for this recipe are on the companion DVD.

grilled monterey bay salmon
with achiote rice-stuffed chiles,
grilled prawn salsa and cilantro-jalapeño crème

MAKES **6 SERVINGS**

6 (6- to 8-ounce) salmon fillets
6 roasted poblano chiles
    Achiote Rice (recipe follows)
    Grilled Prawn Salsa (recipe follows)
    Cilantro-Jalapeño Crème (recipe follows)

Grill salmon over moderate heat until desired doneness.

Stuff roasted poblano chiles with Achiote Rice. Serve alongside salmon, Grilled Prawn Salsa and Cilantro-Jalapeño Crème.

Grilled Prawn Salsa

½ tablespoon garlic
½ tablespoon olive oil
½ teaspoon ground cumin
8 prawns
1 cup diced yellow tomato
1 cup diced red tomato
¼ cup chopped cilantro
½ cup diced red onion
    Juice of 2 limes
    Salt and pepper, to taste

Mix garlic, olive oil, cumin and prawns. Grill prawns until cooked through; dice. Mix with tomatoes, cilantro, onion, lime juice, salt and pepper.

Achiote Rice

1 cup diced yellow onions
1 tablespoon butter
1½ cups medium grain rice
3 cups water or chicken stock
¼ cup achiote chile paste
1½ cups grated Oaxaca cheese
¼ cup chopped fresh cilantro
½ cup chopped green onions
    Juice of 2 limes
1 teaspoon salt

Sweat onions in butter until soft. Add rice with water or chicken stock and achiote paste. Bring to a boil, and then reduce to a simmer and cover. Cook rice 20 to 25 minutes. After rice is cooked and still hot, fold in cheese until melted; cool. Fold in cilantro, green onions, lime juice and salt.

Cilantro-Jalapeño Crème

2 cups sour cream or crème fraîche
1 bunch fresh cilantro, chopped
1 jalapeño pepper
    Juice of 1 lime
    Salt and pepper, to taste

Combine all ingredients in blender and purée until smooth. Strain through fine mesh sieve; reserve.

Sam Marvin

Chef Sam Marvin is a native of Los Angeles. He began his cooking career after studying at Le Cordon Bleu in Paris. Spending seven years abroad, Chef Marvin worked at a number of restaurants throughout the world, from France to Switzerland to Thailand to Morocco to Holland. In addition to dozens of Hollywood celebrities, Marvin has cooked for President Reagan and French President Francois Mitterand.

moroccan breakfast

MAKES **4 SERVINGS**

12	pork breakfast sausages
1	onion
1	green bell pepper
1	red bell pepper
8	cloves garlic, sliced
6	tomatoes
1	can (12 ounces) tomatoes in juice
	Chopped fresh oregano, to taste
	Hot sauce, to taste
	Salt and pepper, to taste
8	eggs

Roughly chop sausage, dice onion and peppers and sauté in large skillet for about 3 minutes. Add garlic to skillet. Chop tomatoes and add to skillet. About 5 minutes later, add canned tomatoes, fresh oregano, hot sauce, salt and pepper. Cover and let simmer lightly for at least 20 minutes and up to 40 minutes. Uncover and crack eggs into stewed mixture; cover and cook 3 minutes. Uncover and serve 2 eggs and one-fourth of stew per person.

Video instructions for this recipe are on the companion DVD.

stuffed pork chops
with tomato salad

MAKES 4 SERVINGS

Pork Chop

4   (12-ounce) center-cut pork loin chops, Frenched

8   thin slices prosciutto

8   slices provolone cheese

8   Fresh sage leaves

    Salt and pepper, to taste

    Extra-virgin olive oil

    Tomato Salad (recipe follows)

Preheat oven to 375°F. Make incision on 1 side of each pork chop. Layer 2 pieces prosciutto, provolone and sage; fold once and insert in pork chop. Repeat stuffing for other chops. Season with salt and pepper and rub with olive oil. Cook in skillet on both sides to get nice color, about 4 minutes on each side. Finish in oven 10 to 12 minutes. Serve with Tomato Salad.

Tomato Salad

8   tomatoes, diced (use a variety of colors and sizes)

8   cloves garlic, finely chopped

1   handful fresh basil, julienned

1   large red onion, sliced thin

    A few dashes red wine vinegar

    Extra-virgin olive oil

    Salt and pepper, to taste

Mix all ingredients in large bowl. Add red wine vinegar, extra-virgin olive oil and seasonings to taste. Squeeze mixture with hands so tomatoes let out all juices. Season again if needed. Can be made 1 day ahead of time.

James Mbugua

Chef James Mbunga's cooking style is inspired by his native Kenya. Two years after arriving in the United States, he graduated from Los Angeles Trade Technical College. He next attended California State Polytechnic University in Pomona, where he was elected to represent the hotel and restaurant department student body at the National Restaurant Association meeting. He has won numerous culinary and food service scholarships.

easter asparagus and ham bake

MAKES **2 SERVINGS**

½	teaspoon olive oil
1	tablespoon chopped shallots
10	ounces asparagus, cut into fourths
10	ounces cooked ham, cut into ¼-inch cubes
1	tablespoon butter or margarine
1	tablespoon all-purpose flour
½	cup milk
¼	cup shredded Cheddar cheese
¼	cup shredded Gruyère cheese
½	cup chopped tomato
⅛	teaspoon dried thyme
¼	cup bread crumbs
	Ground red pepper, to taste

Preheat oven to 375°F. Heat oil in skillet and sauté shallots. Place shallots with asparagus and ham in small casserole dish. Melt butter in saucepan over medium heat; blend in flour. Cook 30 seconds, stirring constantly. Gradually stir in milk. Heat, stirring constantly, until thickened. Stir in remaining ingredients except bread crumbs; heat until cheese is melted. Spoon over ham and asparagus mixture. Bake 15 to 20 minutes or until lightly browned. Remove from oven and sprinkle with bread crumbs. Serve hot.

grilled asparagus and hearty vegetables

MAKES 4 SERVINGS

10 ounces asparagus, cleaned and trimmed
2 teaspoons olive oil
½ teaspoon dried thyme
2 tomatoes, cut in half
1 green bell pepper, cut into ½-inch strips
1 red bell pepper, cut into ½-inch strips
1 yellow bell pepper, cut into ½-inch strips
Salt and pepper, to taste

Heat grill to medium.

Season asparagus with olive oil, thyme, salt and pepper. Place diagonally on grill and cook until grill marks are visible (4 to 5 minutes). Turn over and repeat.

Season tomatoes and place on grill, cut side down. Cook until grill marks are visible. Repeat for bell peppers.

Place asparagus on large plate and garnish with additional grilled vegetables. Serve hot.

Brandon Miller

Executive Chef Brandon Miller of Monterey, California's historic Stokes Restaurant & Bar is a native San Franciscan. His distinguished culinary resume includes an apprenticeship with French Master Chef Georges Blanc; he also worked at Campton Place and LuLu restaurants in San Francisco.

coco pazzo
"crazy strawberries"

MAKES 8 SERVINGS

2	pints fresh strawberries
¼	cup balsamic vinegar
1	tablespoon fresh lemon juice
2	tablespoons sugar
½	teaspoon cracked black pepper
1	quart vanilla bean ice cream or whipped cream and chocolate biscotti

Wash, hull and quarter strawberries. Combine balsamic vinegar, lemon juice, sugar and cracked black pepper in medium bowl. Add strawberries and marinate up to 30 minutes. Taste and adjust seasonings depending on ripeness of fruit. Serve family style with ice cream scooped on top of plate individually or with whipped cream and chocolate biscotti.

Video instructions for this recipe are on the companion DVD.

strawberry tart

MAKES **1 (10-INCH) TART**

½   **cup (1 stick) unsalted butter**
1   **cup all-purpose flour**
2   **to 3 tablespoons ice water**
    Pinch salt
½   **cup strawberry jam, heated**
2   **pint freshstrawberries, hulled**
1   **cup crème fraîche**

Preheat oven to 400°F. Cut butter into small pieces and place in freezer 5 minutes. In bowl of food processor, combine flour, salt and butter. Process 10 seconds until mixture has texture of cornmeal. Add water and process 10 more seconds. Place mixture on wood surface. With heel of hand, incorporate butter and flour into smooth dough. Flatten dough into disk, wrap with plastic wrap and refrigerate 15 minutes. Flour your work surface and rolling pin. Roll dough into 13-inch circle. Line 10-inch tart pan with dough and trim excess. Prick bottom of crust with fork and line with foil. Fill with pie weights and bake 15 minutes, remove beans and complete baking 10 to 15 minutes more to fully bake crust. Let cool.

Brush crust with jam. Dip each strawberry in warm jam and fill crust. Serve with crème fraîche.

Jeff Mosher

Executive Chef Jeff Mosher discovered his interest in the culinary world while working in a local pizzeria as he finished his bachelor's degree at Oberlin College in Oberlin, Ohio. After graduation, Chef Mosher moved to San Francisco and began working as a line cook. After moving up the ranks in various restaurants, he moved to Napa Valley, the epicenter of food and wine. He was named Executive Chef of Julia's Kitchen in 2006.

heirloom tomato, fresh mozzarella and basil salad

MAKES **6 SERVINGS**

1	bunch fresh basil
6	large heirloom tomatoes
1	pound fresh mozzarella cheese
½	pound mixed green lettuce
	Salt and pepper
	Balsamic Vinaigrette (recipe follows)
	Fresh Pesto (recipe follows)

Slice heirloom tomatoes and mozzarella horizontally into ½-inch slices. Place 1 tomato slice on each plate and season with salt and pepper. Place 1 mozzarella slice on each tomato. Place 1 large leaf (or 2 small leaves) basil on mozzarella. Repeat until desired height is reached, 4 to 5 layers. Slice stack and turn to show cut sides. Dress lettuce with Balsamic Vinaigrette and season with salt and pepper to taste. Pile on tomatoes. Drizzle with Fresh Pesto.

Balsamic Vinaigrette

1	tablespoon minced shallots
¼	cup balsamic vinegar
¾	cup olive oil

Mash minced shallots in balsamic vinegar; let stand 10 minutes. Whisk in remaining ¾ cup olive oil and season with salt and pepper.

Fresh Pesto

4	bunches fresh basil
1	tablespoon toasted pine nuts
1	teaspoon minced garlic
½	cup olive oil

Blanch basil in salted water 30 seconds. Shock in ice water bath. When cool, squeeze all water out of basil. Purée in blender with pine nuts, minced garlic and olive oil. Add salt and pepper to taste.

Video instructions for this recipe are on the companion DVD.

basil fettuccini
with heirloom tomato and zucchini ragoût

MAKES **4 SERVINGS**

Heirloom Tomato and Zucchini Ragoût

- 6 heirloom tomatoes
- 1 pint Sungold or cherry tomatoes, quartered
- 5 tablespoons extra-virgin olive oil, divided
- 2 tablespoons minced shallots
- 1 tablespoon minced garlic
- 2 large zucchini, diced
- 3 tablespoons chopped fresh basil, divided
  Basil Fettuccini (recipe follows)
- ¼ cup grated Parmesan cheese

Score heirloom tomatoes, and then blanch in salted water 10 seconds. Cool on sheet tray in refrigerator 10 minutes. When cool, quarter, peel and seed tomatoes. Dice tomatoes.

Heat 4 tablespoons extra-virgin olive oil in large skillet. Add shallots and garlic; sauté 2 minutes or until soft but not brown. Add zucchini and cook additional 2 minutes. Add diced tomatoes, Sungold tomatoes and 2 tablespoons basil. Season and set aside.

Blanch Basil Fettucini in salted water 2 to 3 minutes. When tender, strain and toss with remaining 1 tablespoon extra-virgin olive oil so pasta does not stick together. Divide three-fourths vegetable ragoût among 6 large pasta bowls. Divide pasta among bowls. Top with remaining vegetable ragoût. Garnish with remaining tablespoon of basil and Parmesan cheese.

Pasta

- 3½ cups all-purpose flour
- 4 extra-large eggs
- ½ teaspoon extra-virgin olive oil
- 3 tablespoons chopped fresh basil
  Pinch salt

Combine flour and eggs with electric mixer fitted with dough-hook attachment. Add olive oil, basil and salt. If dry, add touch of water. Wrap dough in plastic wrap and place in refrigerator 1 hour.

Roll dough into long thin sheets using pasta machine. Sprinkle dough with flour if it begins to stick. Attach cutter to machine and cut pasta into ½-inch wide strips. Run thin sheets through cutter and sprinkle noodles with additional flour so they do not stick together. Cut pasta into 1-foot strands. Refrigerate until ready to use.

lobster al' americaine

MAKES 6 SERVINGS

4   celery stalks, chopped
2   yellow onions, chopped
2   leeks, chopped
1   clove garlic, crushed
¼   bunch fresh basil
¼   bunch fresh parsley
1   tablespoon kosher salt
1   fennel bulb, chopped
¼   teaspoon coriander seed
¼   teaspoon fennel seed
⅛   teaspoon white peppercorns
2   cups dry white wine
3   (1¼-pound) lobsters, claws and tails removed; reserve bodies
    Beurre Fondue (recipe follows)
    Risotto (recipe follows)
    Tomato Concassé (recipe follows)
    Fresh tarragon leaves (optional)

Place all ingredients except lobster, Beurre Fondue, Risotto, Tomato Concassé and tarragon in 3-quart saucepan and bring to a boil; reduce to a simmer. Place lobster claws and tails in pot 5 minutes. Remove and place in ice bath. Place lobster bodies in pot 3½ minutes. Remove and place in ice water. Crack claws and tails and remove meat. Cut tail meat in half. Reserve poaching liquid for Risotto, and reserve lobster bodies and roe for use in Tomato Concassé.

Poach lobster meat in simmering Beurre Fondue until just firm. Mound Risotto in center of 6 bowls, and then arrange half a lobster tail and meat from 1 claw on top of Risotto in each bowl. Blend Tomato Concassé with Buerre Fondue and pour over lobster and around rice. Garnish with fresh tarragon leaves and serve.

Beurre Fondue

½   cup dry white wine
½   cup (1 stick) butter
1½ quarts water

Bring all ingredients to boil in small saucepan, and then reduce heat to simmer. Season with salt.

Risotto

1   tablespoon butter
½   yellow onion, diced
1   cup arborio rice
2   bay leaves
¼   cup dry white wine
6   cups hot chicken stock (or court bouillon from poaching lobster)

Melt butter in large saucepan. Add onion and cook until translucent. Add rice and sauté until golden brown. Add bay leaves and white wine. Stir in ½ cup stock; cook and stir until stock is absorbed. Repeat with remaining stock.

Tomato Concassé

1   tablespoon canola oil (or other neutral oil)
1   bulb fennel, chopped
1   leek, chopped
1   yellow onion, peeled and chopped
1   carrot, peeled and chopped
3   celery stalks, chopped
4   tomatoes, cored and scored on bottoms
    Lobster bodies and roe, from above
¼   cup brandy
2   tablespoons vermouth
3   cups water
¼   cup (½ stick) butter

Heat canola oil in saucepan and add leek, yellow onion, carrot and celery. Once browned, crush lobster bodies and add bodies and roe to pan. Sauté until lobster shells are red. Add tomatoes and cook 2 minutes.

Deglaze with brandy and vermouth and reduce by half; add water and simmer. Reduce by two-thirds and strain through fine strainer into deep bowl or saucepan. Blend in butter with hand blender and season to taste with salt and pepper.

Christian Mueller & Dawn Pliche

Chef Christian Mueller is the Executive Chef at Ducey's on the Lake in Bass Lake, California.

Chef Dawn Pliche is the head sous chef and kitchen manager at Ducey's. Prior to joining Ducey's, she worked as a caterer for the motion picture industry, making sure the actors' and directors' dietary needs were met.

honey plum chicken

MAKES 1 SERVING

¼ cup clarified butter (see Note)
1 (7-ounce) chicken breast, lightly pounded and floured
1 teaspoon minced garlic
1 teaspoon chopped shallot
2 tablespoons chopped red bell pepper
¼ cup orange-flavored liqueur
2 tablespoons white wine
1 tablespoon honey
2 plums, diced
1 tablespoon butter

Heat clarified butter in medium skillet and add chicken breast. Lightly brown breast about 1 minute on each side. Add garlic, shallot and bell pepper and cook about 1 minute. Add orange-flavored liqueur and white wine. Reduce 1 minute. Add honey, plums and butter. Arrange chicken breast on plate and pour plum sauce over it.

Note: To clarify butter, slowly melt ½ pound (2 sticks) unsalted butter in skillet or saucepan. After butter is melted let sit a short while. Foam and milk solids will sink to bottom of pan; clarified butter is left on top. Carefully pour it out of pot into container, taking care that milk solids do not mix back in.

plum dumplings

MAKES 4 SERVINGS

8   plums, preferably Damsons
8   sugar cubes
1   pound all-purpose flour
1   pound baker's cheese (see note below)
2   eggs
    Pinch salt
    Granulated sugar
    Cinnamon
    Melted unsalted butter

Rinse plums and remove pits without halving them (coring plums from top). Stuff each plum with 1 sugar cube. Combine flour, baker's cheese, eggs and salt and knead into smooth dough. Divide dough into 8 portions and flatten each portion between palms of hands. Wrap dough portions around each plum and roll between palms of your hands to smooth. (Plums should only be covered by thin layer of dough.) Drop dumplings in boiling water and simmer 20 minutes. Using a perforated spoon, carefully remove dumplings from the water. Sprinkle dumplings with mixture of sugar and cinnamon. Serve with melted butter.

plum gratin

MAKES 4 SERVINGS

6   large plums
3   eggs
½   cup honey
½   vanilla bean, split and scraped
½   pound baker's cheese (see note below)
    Zest and juice of 1 lemon

Preheat oven to 375°F. Rinse and halve plums. Remove pits. Cut each half into 4 wedges. Separate eggs; whip whites to stiff peaks. Beat yolks, honey and vanilla with electric mixer until foamy. Add baker's cheese, lemon juice and zest and whip until incorporated. Carefully fold in egg whites. Divide batter into 4 ovenproof forms. Arrange plum wedges on batter in each circle. Push wedges gently into batter so they are half covered. Bake about 15 minutes or until browned.

Chef's note: Baker's cheese is an unripened soft cheese commonly used by commercial bakeries to make fillings for pastries since it stays moist even after baking. Baker's cheese may be ordered from the cheese counter at specialty grocery stores and cheese markets or from various sources online. You may substitute another unripened soft cheese such as ricotta, farmer's cheese, cream cheese or even cottage cheese if first you wrap it in several layers of damp cheese cloth and squeeze it to remove as much liquid as possible.

Dee Nguyen

Chef Dee Nguyen is the chef and owner of Break of Dawn restaurant in Laguna Hills, California. As the former sous chef at the Ritz-Carlton, Laguna Niguel, he was on the fast track in the professional cooking world. A family matter caused him to reevaluate his priorities, and Chef Nguyen left the Ritz-Carlton. He opened Break of Dawn—a brunch restaurant—which allows him to spend more time with his family.

avocado and mango smoothie

MAKES **4 SERVINGS**

1 avocado, peeled and pit removed
1 mango, peeled and cut away from seed
2 cups crushed ice
3 tablespoons condensed milk
½ cup coconut milk (or plain yogurt)
2 tablespoons rum (optional)

Cut avocado in half lengthwise; remove pit and scoop out pulp. Peel mango and cut away fruit from hard seed in middle. Combine all ingredients in blender and blend well.

spiced pork chop
with avocado and pomegranate salad

MAKES 4 SERVINGS

1 tablespoon chopped shallots
1 teaspoon chopped garlic
1 teaspoon chopped ginger
1 cup pomegranate juice
2 tablespoons soy sauce
2 tablespoons brown sugar
¼ cup extra-virgin olive oil
4 (10-ounce) pork chops
1 teaspoon ground cloves
1 teaspoon ground allspice
1 teaspoon ground black pepper
Salt, to taste
¼ cup (½ stick) butter, cut into pieces
Avocado and Pomegranate Salad
  (recipe follows)
Sautéed Arugula (recipe follows)

Combine shallots, garlic, ginger, pomegranate juice, soy sauce, brown sugar and olive oil. Marinate pork chops in mixture overnight.

Preheat oven to 350°F. Remove pork chops from marinade and save juice for sauce. Season chops with cloves, allspice, black pepper and salt. Sear chops on medium-high heat until golden. Finish chops in oven about 15 minutes or until internal temperature is 145°F. Remove chops from pan and let them rest. Add marinade juice to pan and reduce by one-third. Turn off heat and slowly whisk in butter. Season to taste. Serve with Avocado and Pomegranate Salad and Sautéed Arugula.

Avocado and Pomegranate Salad
1 Haas avocado, diced
½ pomegranate, seeds only (cleaned)
1 cucumber, diced
1 teaspoon chopped fresh ginger
¼ red onion, diced
1 tablespoon extra-virgin olive oil
  Grated peel and juice of 1 lime
1 tablespoon chopped fresh mint
1 tablespoon sour cream
  Salt and pepper, to taste

Combine all ingredients and toss. Season with salt and pepper.

Sautéed Arugula
4 cups arugula
1 teaspoon chopped shallot
1 teaspoon chopped garlic
  Extra-virgin olive oil

Sauté arugula with oil, shallot and garlic. Season to taste.

James Ormsby

Executive Chef James Ormsby of PlumpJack Café in San Francisco was named "Best Chef in San Francisco" in 1999. His love for food began while growing up in Oakland, California. At the age of 14, he entered the culinary industry, beginning as a dish washer at a local coffee shop. For the next 15 years, he mastered his cooking-style and technique by working in a variety of restaurants. In 2000, he joined the team at PlumpJack Café.

baby new potatoes
with caviar and crème fraîche

MAKES **3 DOZEN APPETIZERS**

18 small new potatoes
3 tablespoons butter, melted
Salt and black pepper, to taste
¾ cup crème fraîche
2 ounces caviar*
2 tablespoons minced chives

Note: Good quality black caviar tastes best in this dish, but an assortment of caviar is fun and more affordable.

Clean potatoes well and place in large pot with cold salted water on high heat. Bring potatoes to a boil; turn heat to a simmer. Cook until potatoes are just tender, about 10 to 15 minutes depending on size. Drain and let cool in colander to steam off any moisture.

Cut potatoes in half. Slice off ends of potatoes to allow them to sit on plate without wobbling. With small spoon or melon baller, take small scoop out of potato to hold crème fraîche and caviar.

Toss potato halves with melted butter and add salt and pepper.

Arrange potatoes on serving platter and top each with 1 teaspoon crème fraîche. Top with caviar and sprinkle with chives.

Serve warm.

crushed new red and white potatoes

with fresh dungeness crab and meyer lemon butter

MAKES **4 SERVINGS**

12 new red potatoes
12 new white potatoes
    Juice of 2 Meyer lemons
    Zest of 1 Meyer lemon
 2 sticks (1 cup) unsalted butter
 2 tablespoons crème fraîche
 1 teaspoon salt
    Black pepper, to taste
 1 fresh large Dungeness crab,
    cooked and cleaned, or 1
    pound fresh crabmeat
 ¼ cup minced fresh chives, plus
    extra for garnish

Place cleaned potatoes in plenty of cold, salted water (add 1 tablespoon salt per quart water). Bring water to a boil and cook, covered, 15 to 20 minutes or until potatoes are soft. Drain and let air dry 1 minute.

Cover with towel to keep warm while making sauce.

Warm lemon juice and zest over medium heat and whisk in butter and crème fraîche a bit at a time.

Season with salt and pepper; add crab and chives. Keep warm.

Place potatoes in shallow bowl. Use spatula to gently crush and break open potatoes. Spoon crab sauce over open potatoes. Serve hot.

Garnish with freshly ground black pepper and chives.

Chefs note: For special occasions, substitute fresh lobster meat for Dungeness crab and garnish with caviar instead of chives.

Video instructions for this recipe are on the companion DVD.

ahi cones

MAKES **8 SERVINGS**

4   sheets feuilles de briks*
    Olive oil
1   teaspoon black sesame seeds
½   pound sashimi-grade ahi tuna
2   tablespoons grated fresh horseradish
2   tablespoons chopped capers
2   tablespoons minced fresh chives
    Grated peel and juice of 1 lime
1   tablespoon whole grain mustard
1   teaspoon Worcestershire sauce
1   teaspoon hot pepper sauce
2   tablespoons minced shallots
2   tablespoons extra-virgin olive oil
3   tablespoons tobiko caviar
    Salt and pepper, to taste

Note: Feuilles de briks (literally "Leaves of Dough") is often available in ethnic grocery stores, and with the frozen doughs in some grocery stores. Quality products can be ordered from online sources, too. If a source cannot be found, you may substitute a sheet of filo dough brushed with melted butter and folded in half for each half sheet of feuilles de briks, but results may differ.

Tools

8   3½-inch lady lock metal cream horn
    molds
1   pastry brush

Feuilles de briks are circular. Place tip of mold in center of leaf; roll mold in circle to measure how big leaf should be to fit mold. Trim leaf to smaller circle; cut that circle in half.

Preheat oven to 350°F. Brush lightly with olive oil and sprinkle with black sesame seeds. Roll sphere around mold to make an even cone shape. Place seam down on metal cookie sheet (mold keeps it

from unraveling). Do not wrap dough too tight, or it will be difficult to take off mold. Bake 8 minutes or until golden brown. Cones can be stored in airtight container about 1 week.

Dice ahi into small cubes; ahi should be free of all sinew. Combine horseradish, capers, chives, lime peel and juice, mustard, Worcestershire sauce, hot pepper sauce, shallots and olive oil. Add to diced tuna. Add salt and pepper. Place gently into cones. Top with caviar. Serve.

Pierre Padovani & David Passanisi

Chef Pierre Padovani studied pastry and cooked in restaurants in France before moving to Hawaii. He oversees production of Padovani's Chocolates and cooks at Padovani's Restaurant and Wine Bar.

Chef David Passanisi is a graduate of the New England Culinary Institute. He worked at some of the best restaurants in Boston before he moved to Hawaii in 2002 and began working at Padovani's in 2003.

roasted muscovy duck breast on okinawan sweet potato purée
with ginger jus, spiced apples, braised endives and pan-fried plums

MAKES **4 SERVINGS**

4   Muscovy duck breasts (1 pound each)
    Salt and white pepper, to taste
    Okinawan Sweet Potato Purée (recipe follows)
    Braised Endives (recipe follows)
    Spiced Apple Compote (recipe follows)
    Ginger Jus (recipe follows)
    Pan Fried Plums (recipe follows)

Generously salt fatty side of duck breasts. Cook fat side down in heavy frying pan over low heat 9 minutes. Turn duck breasts over to sear skin side; cook 3 minutes more. Remove from pan; set aside and keep warm.

Spoon 2 quenelles Okinawan Sweet Potato Purée on each of 4 warmed plates. Place 1 Braised Endive half on each plate next to potatoes. Place ½ cup Spiced Apple Compote on each plate. Pour ¼ cup Ginger Jus on each plate, avoiding purée, endive and compote. Slice each duck breast into 8 slices and arrange over sauce on a plate. Add 1 Pan Fried Plum to each plate and serve immediately.

Okinawan Sweet Potato Purée
1   pound Okinawan sweet potatoes
    Salt, to taste
¼   cup (½ stick) butter
¼   cup milk
¼   cup cream

Peel sweet potatoes, cut into quarters and cook in boiling salt water until soft. Drain and process with food mill. Return to pot and vigorously stir butter into purée. Add just enough boiling milk and cream, a little at a time, until a purée is thick and stiff. Keep warm in pot or double boiler on stove until serving.

Braised Endives

2 large Belgian endives
3 tablespoons butter
Pinch sugar
Chicken stock or water
Salt and white pepper, to taste

Remove any discolored outer leaves from endives. Cut off root ends and any green on tops. Melt butter in large skillet over high heat. Add endive and cook until warmed but not browned. Add stock to barely cover, and continue to cook on high heat until stock and butter have reduced to a glaze and endive is cooked. Season with salt and white pepper.

Spiced Apple Compote

2 cups water
½ cup sugar
1½ teaspoons curry powder
½ teaspoon ground turmeric
½ teaspoon saffron powder
1 pinch saffron threads
3 cardamom pods
2 teaspoons lemon juice
1 tablespoon butter
½ vanilla bean, split and scraped
3¼ pounds apples, peeled, cored and sliced
Salt and white pepper, to taste
½ cup chopped fresh cilantro

Bring all ingredients except apples, salt, pepper and cilantro to a boil. After 2 minutes add apple. Season to taste with salt and pepper. Cook until apples are soft and liquid thickens slightly. Stir in cilantro to finish.

Ginger Jus

¼ cup Kiawe honey*
2 tablespoons fresh ginger
¼ cup Jerez sherry vinegar
1 cup brown chicken stock
2 tablespoons butter
Salt and white pepper, to taste

Note: Kiawe (pronounced "kee AH vay") honey is produced by bees using only the nectar from blossoms of the kiawe tree, which only grows in Hawaii. Kiawe honey can be ordered from sources online, or substitute your favorite honey variety.

Heat honey and ginger in pan until caramelized. Deglaze with vinegar. Reduce 2 to 3 minutes; add chicken stock. Bring to a boil and reduce to one-third original volume. Whisk in butter, season to taste and strain through fine sieve. Keep warm until needed.

Pan-Fried Plums

1 tablespoon butter
2 plums, cut into halves then fans

Melt butter in large skillet; sauté plums a few minutes until cooked through.

Charles Paladin-Wayne

Chef Charles Paladin-Wayne began cooking professionally in 1972 in Phoenix, Arizona. After working his way up to Regional Kitchen Supervisor for a company overseeing more than 500 restaurants throughout the United States, he left to work in the kitchens of restaurants up and down the California coast. He left the restaurant business in 1997 to work for wineries such as Edna Valley, Justin Vineyards, and Summerwood Winery and now operates his own catering business.

122

thompson seedless grapes
with cypress gardens chèvre, roasted walnuts and prosciutto

MAKES **6 SERVINGS**

2   pounds chèvre (goat cheese)
1   pound walnuts
2   pounds Thompson seedless grapes or other seedless varieties, stemmed and cleaned (approximately 30 to 40 grapes)
15   to 20 thin slices prosciutto, cut in half lengthwise

Set out cheese to soften on parchment paper. Cover with plastic wrap so it does not dry out. Toast and chop walnuts. Sift walnuts in large wire strainer to remove small, dust-like particles of chopped walnut.

Moisten hands and roll 1 grape in chèvre, coating grape thickly. Wrap prosciutto around cheese-covered grape (use toothpick to hold together, if necessary). Dip top and bottom in chopped walnuts and set on serving platter. Repeat with remaining ingredients. Refrigerate 30 minutes, or cover with plastic wrap and refrigerate until serving.

Chef's Note: Wet your hands on a damp towel frequently to keep cheese from sticking to your hands.

lavender sugared grapes
with verjus sorbet

MAKES **6 SERVINGS**

3   cups verjus
1   tablespoon lemon juice
1   cup granulated sugar
4   egg whites
    Lavender Sugar (recipe
    follows)
18 seedless red flame grapes,
    stemmed, cleaned and dried
    Fresh mint leaves (optional)

*Note: Verjus (sometimes called "verjuice") is the juice of unripe grapes. It has a sour, acidic flavor often compared to lemon juice or vinegar. Some wineries sell verjus directly to consumers, as do several online sources.

Cook verjus, lemon juice and granulated sugar in medium saucepan over medium heat until sugar dissolves and mixture is hot, but not boiling. Refrigerate until completely cool.

Follow manufacturer's instructions to make sorbet if using ice cream maker. If not, pour cooled juice into 9-inch square baking pan and freeze, stirring occasionally with fork to break up ice crystals. When fully frozen, transfer to food processor and pulse until slushy; cover and refreeze to allow flavors to ripen. For best results, sorbet should be prepared at least 1 day before serving.

Place egg whites and lavender sugar in separate bowls. Dip 1 grape into egg whites and then roll in sugar, coating grape well. Set on paper towel-lined sheet pan and repeat with remaining grapes. Set aside to dry at least 1 hour.

Check sorbet for consistency and reprocess if necessary. Spoon sorbet into ice cream dish or martini glass and place 3 or more grapes on top. Garnish with mint. Serve immediately.

Luke Patterson

Chef Luke Patterson is the executive chef at the restaurant at the Crosby Golf Club in Rancho Santa Fe, California. He is the former executive chef of La Valencia Hotel in La Jolla, California and has more than 17 years of culinary experience throughout California.

seared ahi
with banana and avocado salsa

MAKES **2 SERVINGS**

- 2 tablespoons olive oil
- 6 ounces sashimi-grade ahi tuna
- 1 teaspoon salt
- 1 teaspoon white pepper
  Banana and Avocado Salsa (recipe follows)

Heat olive oil until smoking in large skillet. Season tuna with salt and pepper. Sear on all sides in olive oil. Inside should be rare. Remove from pan and let rest. Slice into ½-inch-thick slices and serve, topped with Banana and Avocado Salsa.

Banana and Avocado Salsa

- 1 banana, sliced
- ¼ avocado, diced
- ¼ red bell pepper, diced
- 3 tablespoons fresh orange juice
  Juice of ½ lime
- 2 teaspoons minced fresh cilantro
- 2 teaspoons chopped green onion
- 1 teaspoon diced fresh ginger
  Salt and pepper, to taste

Place all ingredients in bowl and let stand at least 10 minutes. Serve with Seared Ahi or chips, bread or crackers.

hawaiian sweet bread french toast

with caramelized bananas and vanilla-vodka coconut syrup

MAKES **2 SERVINGS**

2　tablespoons sugar
2　bananas, sliced
½　can piña colada coconut drink mix
½　can coconut milk
¼　cup vodka
2　eggs
1　teaspoon vanilla extract
½　cup milk
4　slices Hawaiian sweet bread, sliced ½ inch thick
2　tablespoons butter
2　ounces macadamia nuts, chopped and toasted

Cook sugar until amber in large skillet over medium heat. Add bananas. Cook 2 minutes or until soft and coated with caramelized sugar. Set aside, keeping warm. In separate skillet, cook piña colada mix and coconut milk until reduced by half and syrupy. Stir in vodka. Set aside, keeping warm. Beat eggs, vanilla and milk in bowl. Melt butter in clean, large skillet; dip 2 slices bread in egg batter and fry in butter until golden brown on both sides. Transfer to plate and top with half the bananas, some vodka-coconut syrup and half the macadamia nuts. Repeat with remaining bread.

banana-mango smoothie

MAKES **2 SERVINGS**

2　bananas
½　cup pineapple juice
½　cup fresh orange juice
1　cup ice
3　tablespoons milk
¾　cup mango sorbet

Blend all ingredients until smooth.

Tom Perini

Chef Tom Perini grew up on the Perini Ranch in Buffalo Gap, Texas. His official culinary career began as a chuck wagon cook back in 1973. Ten years after cooking at the wagon, he opened Perini Ranch Steakhouse on his family's working ranch.

Chef Perini's career soared when he introduced his mesquite smoked peppered beef tenderloin—Tom liked the recipe so much, that in 1995, he set out to market it as a mail-order item. Since its introduction, tens of thousands of tenderloin have been sold.

After catering a Texas-themed event for the National Arboretum in Washington, DC, Chef Perini was approached to write a cookbook

on his Texas-style cooking. In 2000, he introduced his coffee-table-style cookbook, Texas Cowboy Cooking. The cookbook features his recipes, cooking tips, and how to select the right cut of beef.

With his unique style of cooking, along with his naturally engagning Texas demeanor, he has gained national and international attention. He has appeared on many national morning television news programs, speaking about his authentic, classic Texas-style of cooking.

One of the chef's highest honors was being invited—six times—to cook at New York's James Beard House. He has

traveled internationally to promote U.S. beef and has offered chef's seminars utilizing U.S. beef in Europe and Asia.

And yet, despite his growing national and international fame, Chef Perini still stays true to his home state, enjoying his spending time on his ranch and remaining active in the community that helped start his career.

navajo tacos

MAKES 8 SERVINGS

1   pound lean ground beef
½   teaspoon ground cumin
½   teaspoon garlic salt
1   jar (16 ounces) Pace® Fire-Roasted Tomato Chunky Salsa
1   package (17 ounces) refrigerated extra-large biscuits (containing 8 biscuits)
    Vegetable oil
    Assorted garnish such as guacamole, shredded lettuce, chopped onion, chopped tomato, shredded Cheddar cheese and chunky salsa

COOK beef in skillet until no longer pink. Add cumin, garlic salt and fire-roasted tomato salsa. Heat to a boil. Cook over low heat 10 minutes.

ROLL out or pat biscuits into 7-inch rounds on floured surface. Place rounds on floured baking sheets.

HEAT ½-inch oil in skillet over medium heat to 375°F. Fry each round for 1 minute or until golden brown, turning once. Drain on paper towels.

PLACE some beef mixture down center of each bread. Garnish as desired.

smoky chipotle cowboy chili

MAKES **4 SERVINGS**

1 pound ground beef
2 cloves garlic, minced
1 tablespoon chili powder
1 can (15 ounces) red kidney beans, rinsed and drained
1 cup chunky chipotle salsa
1 cup frozen whole kernel corn
1 can (14 ounces) seasoned beef broth with onion

Cook beef, garlic and chili powder in saucepan over mediiu-high heat until beef is no longer pink. Pour off drippings.

Stir in beans, salsa, corn and broth. Bring to a boil. Reduce heat to low and simmer 15 minutes. Serve with Cornbread Squares.

Cornbread Squares

1 package (about 8 ounces) corn muffin mix
½ cup picante sauce
½ cup Cheddar cheese, shredded

Preheat oven to 400°F. Prepare corn muffin mix according to package directions.

Spread half the batter in greased 8-inch square baking pan. Top with the salsa and cheese. Spread remaining batter on top. Bake 20 minutes or until done. Cool slightly before serving.

Video instructions for this recipe are on the companion DVD.

caroline's fruit crisp

MAKES **6 TO 8 SERVINGS**

6 to 8 large fresh peaches, peeled and sliced (about 4 cups total)*
  Juice of 1 lemon *or* lime (about 2 tablespoons)
1 tablespoon ground cinnamon, divided
½ cup (1 stick) butter
1 cup all-purpose flour
1 cup light brown sugar
¾ cup chopped pecans (optional)
  Peach Brandy Sauce (recipe follows)
  Vanilla ice cream or sweetened whipped cream (optional)

Note: Substitute 4 cups of another seasonal fruit for peaches when they are unavailable.

Preheat oven to 350°F. Arrange peaches in bottom of 9-inch square baking dish. Sprinkle with the lemon juice and 1½ teaspoons cinnamon.

Combine butter, remaining 1½ teaspoons cinnamon, flour and brown sugar and pecans (if using) in bowl. Mix until combined. Crumble on top of peaches and bake 30 minutes or until brown and bubbly. Serve warm topped with Peach Brandy Sauce and vanilla ice cream or whipped cream.

Peach Brandy Sauce
4 to 5 peaches, peeled
⅓ cup peach brandy

Purée the peaches (you should have 1½ cups purée). Cook with brandy in saucepan over low heat 10 minutes, stirring constantly.

Video instructions for this recipe are on the companion DVD.

Wilhelm Pirngruber

While growing up in Austria, Chef Wilhelm Pirngruber developed a passion for sweets as he helped his mother prepare traditional Austrian desserts. He began his formal chef's training at 15 . Before joining Hilton, he traveled extensively and cooked for dignitaries around the world. Chef Pirngruber's passion for service and Hawaiian-style food has made him Director of Food & Beverage for the Hilton Waikoloa Village and the ambassador of Aloha for the Hawaii Visitors Bureau.

red curry shrimp
in a pineapple

MAKES **1 SERVINGS**

½   tablespoons olive oil
7   shrimp, shell on
⅛   medium onion, cut into 1-inch pieces
1   shiitake mushroom, cleaned and sliced
½   small pineapple, halved, hollowed out, fruit reserved and cut into chunks
⅓   teaspoon red curry paste
¼   cup white wine
½   cup heavy cream
½   cup coconut milk
1½ tablespoons cilantro
1   red potato, cooked and quartered
1   plum tomato, quartered
    Fish sauce, to taste
    Salt, to taste
    Pepper, to taste

Heat olive oil in large skillet and sear shrimp. Remove shrimp. Add onion, mushroom and pineapple chunks to skillet. Add red curry paste. Deglaze with wine and reduce; add cream and reduce. Add remaining ingredients and seared shrimp and adjust seasoning. Serve in reserved pineapple half.

Video instructions for this recipe are on the companion DVD.

macadamia nut baked fresh opakapaka

with mango chutney, pineapple fried wild rice and beurre blanc sauce

MAKES 15 SERVINGS

10 (3-ounce) opakapaka (Hawaiian pink snapper) fillets
¼ cup (½ stick) butter
6 tablespoons chopped fresh cilantro
½ cup Mango Chutney, puréed (recipe follows, or use a pre-made version)
1¼ cups chopped macadamia nuts
  Salt and pepper, to taste
  Pineapple Fried Wild Rice (recipe follows)
  Beurre Blanc Sauce (recipe follows)

1 teaspoon salt
1 teaspoon ground cardamom
1 teaspoon ground coriander
½ teaspoon ground cumin

Preheat oven to 325°F. Season fish fillets with salt and pepper. Heat butter and sear fillets on both sides. Remove from heat.

Stir cilantro into Mango Chutney. Brush fillets with chutney mixture and generously coat with macadamia nuts. Bake 7 to 8 minutes. Serve with Pineapple Fried Wild Rice and drizzle plate with Buerre Blanc Sauce.

Cook mangos and vinegar over low heat in large saucepan 10 minutes. Stir in sugar, ginger, garlic, raisins, redpeppers and salt. Increase heat, bringing slowly to a boil, stirring well. Reduce heat; simmer 30 minutes, stirring occasionally. Remove from heat and stir in remaining ingredients. Chill in ice bath. Store in airtight container. For best flavor, refrigerate 1 month before using.

Mango Chutney *(makes 6 servings)*
6 ripe mangos, peeled, pitted and diced
1¼ cups cider vinegar
1⅓ cups brown sugar
1½ ounces fresh ginger, minced
2 cloves garlic, minced
½ cup raisins
2 teaspoons seeded and chopped red peppers

Pineapple Fried Wild Rice
  (makes 15 servings)
2 tablespoons unsalted butter
⅜ cup diced leek
⅓ cup cooked diced ham
⅜ cup diced red bell pepper
⅜ cup diced yellow bell pepper
¾ cup diced pineapple
½ ounce garlic, minced
¾ cup golden raisins
¾ cup dried cranberries
2 sage leaves, chopped
10 cups cooked wild rice
¾ cup diced and roasted macadamia nuts
5 tablespoons chopped cilantro
  Salt, to taste

Melt butter in large skillet or wok. Add leek and ham; cook and stir until leek softens and ham begins to brown. Add peppers, pineapple, garlic, raisins, cranberries and sage and cook until fragrant. Add cooked wild rice and season to taste with salt and pepper. Serve sprinkled with macadamia nuts and cilantro.

Buerre Blanc Sauce *(makes 10 servings)*

¼	lemon
¼	cup white wine
¼	tablespoon chopped shallot
5	black peppercorn
1	tablespoon heavy cream
½	cup (1 stick) butter, softened
	Salt and white pepper, to taste

Peel lemon and chop pulp. Cook with wine, shallots and black peppercorns in saucepan over medium-low heat until mixture is reduced to 10% of original volume. Stir in cream. Remove from heat and whip in soft butter. Season to taste with salt and white pepper. Strain and keep warm on edge of stove (do not allow to boil or sauce will break and separate).

Note: This is one of the basic sauces of French cuisine often called "mother sauces" because they are the base for so many variations. Beurre blanc can be flavored to your liking with fruit purées, herbs or liquor.

Paul Prudhomme

Chef Paul Prudhomme was raised on a farm near Opelousas in Louisiana's Acadiana country. The youngest of 13 children, he got his first experience cooking at the age of seven, when the last of his sisters left home. While helping his mother in the kitchen, he learned the value of fresh, quality products—since there was no electricity or refrigeration on the farm, they used only what was fresh and in season.

Chef Prudhomme realized at a young age that food preparation was to be his life's work. Upon finishing school, he began to travel, working as a cook in a variety of restaurants where he absorbed everything he could about many regional cooking styles. Eventually he settled in New Orleans. He polished his skills and built a following at a well-known Garden District restaurant.

In 1979, he and his late wife, K Hinrichs Prudhomme, opened a small restaurant on Chartres Street in the French Quarter—K-Paul's Louisiana Kitchen. This was to be a casual dining spot for local customers, but once word of the amazing dishes at the restaurant got out, both locals and tourists flocked in to try some of Chef Prudhomme's creations.

Often appearing on national television, he has become one of the country's most celebrated chefs. His achievements include being the first American-born chef to receive the coveted Merité Agricole of the French Republic, and in 1986, the American Culinary Federation honored him as "Culinarian of the Year." He has written numerous cookbooks and has been featured in such national magazines as Life, Time, Omni, Newsweek, Bon Appetit, Metropolitan Home, and Travel and Leisure. He and his staff have had the opportunity to cook for major events, including President Ronald Reagan's inauguration, the Congressional Barbecue, and many heads of state dinners. Chef Paul Prudhomme is constantly learning and experimenting in his endeavor to create new, delicious recipes.

bronzed chicken breasts
with watermelon sauce

MAKES 4 SERVINGS

Chicken

- **2** tablespoons unsalted butter or margarine, melted
- **4** (3-ounce) boneless, skinless chicken breast halves, at room temperature
- **1** tablspoon plus 1 teaspoon Chef Paul Prudhomme's Poultry Magic®
- Watermelon Sauce (recipe follows)

Preheat heavy nonstick skillet over medium-high heat until hot, about 7 minutes. Pound chicken breasts to ¾ inch thick, if desired. Drizzle both sides of each chicken breast with butter, then sprinkle one side evenly with ½ teaspoon Poultry Magic. Place chicken in skillet seasoned sides down and sprinkle top sides evenly with remaining seasoning blend.

Cook chicken until underside is bronze in color, 2 to 3 minutes. Cook until done, 2 to 3 minutes more. (Do not overcook; chicken should be very juicy.) Top with warm Watermelon Sauce.

Watermelon Sauce *(Makes 1½ Cups)*

- **3** cups seeded and diced watermelon, divided
- **¼** cup cane vinegar
- **¼** cup white balsamic vinegar
- **¼** cup water
- **2** tablespoons sugar
- **2** teaspoons Chef Paul Prudhomme's Pork & Veal Magic®
- **1** cup heavy cream

Combine 1 cup watermelon, cane vinegar, white balsamic vinegar, water, sugar and Pork & Veal Magic. Process until smooth, about 30 seconds. Pour into 10-inch skillet over high heat. Stir well then add the remaining 2 cups of diced watermelon. Bring to a boil then reduce heat to medium and simmer, stirring frequently, until the liquid is reduced to a syrup consistency (about 15 minutes). Stir in cream and return to a boil. Simmer, stirring frequently until the flavors blend and sauce thickens, about 4 minutes. Keep warm over low heat until needed, stirring occasionally to keep sauce from separating.

Video instructions for this recipe are on the companion DVD.

green pizza
with fresh watermelon topping

MAKES 4 SERVINGS

1 tablespoon active dry yeast

1 tablespoon sugar

1½ cups warm water (105°F to 115°F), divided

3½ cups unbleached all-purpose flour

½ cup yellow cornmeal

5 tablespoons, plus 4 teaspoons Chef Paul Prudhomme's Herbal Pizza & Pasta Magic™, divided

4 teaspoons Chef Paul Prudhomme's Pork & Veal Magic®

¼ cup plus 4 teaspoons olive oil, divided

1 cup chopped mustard greens

1 cup chopped chard or kale

2 cups chopped baby spinach

4 cups (about 1 pound) shredded mozzarella cheese

½ cup finely shredded Parmesan cheese

2 tablespoon Watermelon Compote (recipe follows) (optional)

Watermelon wedges (about 3/8-inch thick), cut to fit the pizza slices

Stir yeast and sugar into ½ cup warm water until dissolved. Set aside.

Combine flour, cornmeal, 4 teaspoons Herbal Pizza & Pasta Magic and Pork & Veal Magic in bowl of stand mixer fitted with dough hook attachment. Turn mixer to slow speed and add pour in yeast mixture, remaining 1 cup warm water and ¼ cup olive oil. Increase to medium speed and mix until dough is smooth and elastic and no longer sticks to side of bowl, about 6 to 8 minutes. Turn off mixer. Remove bowl and cover with clean kitchen towel. Let dough rise in warm place until doubled in bulk, about 2 hours.

Preheat oven to 450°F. Place one-fourth dough on floured work surface. Roll out into 8-inch circle, pinching edges to form a thick border. Brush crust and edges with olive oil. Transfer crust to baking sheet. Repeat with remaining dough to form 3 more crusts.

Combine greens, chard, spinach, mozzarella cheese, Parmesan cheese, remaining 5 tablespoons Herbal Pizza & Pasta Magic, remaining 4 teaspoons olive oil and Watermelon Compote; toss well. Spread one-fourth (about 1¾ cups) greens mixture on each crust. Bake until the cheese and crusts are golden brown, 10 to 15 minutes. Just before serving, arrange watermelon wedges on each pizza.

Note: The pizza topping gets an extra dimension of flavor when you add the Watermelon Compote to the mixture, but if you do not want to use the jam, the topping will still taste very good. You may want to use a little less Herbal Pizza & Pasta Magic if you omit the Watermelon Jam.

Watermelon Compote

4 cups seeded and diced (½ inch) watermelon

¼ cup minced fresh ginger

Juice and zest of 1 lime

1½ cups sugar

2 tablespoons Chef Paul Prudhomme's Salmon Magic™

Combine all ingredients except Salmon Magic in large bowl. Stir well, then cover and let rest for two hours, stirring occasionally.

Strain watermelon pieces from liquid, reserving melon and the liquid. Set melon pieces aside.

Cook liquid and Salmon Magic in 10-inch skillet over high heat until boiling. Reduce heat to medium and cook, stirring occasionally, until iquid has reduced by half, about 8 minutes. Add reserved melon pieces. Increase heat to high and cook, stirring frequently, until the mixture is syrupy, about

6 to 8 minutes. Remove from heat and cool. Refrigerate until ready to use.

Chef's Note: To create a very intensely flavored jam, purée the compote in a blender and place in a skillet over high heat. Cook, stirring constantly, until the liquid has reduced by half, and is very thick and syrupy, about 4 minutes. Remove from heat and cool, then cover and refrigerate. The mixture will thicken to a jam consistency as it cools.

Video instructions for this recipe are on the companion DVD.

the angler's wife salad
with pickled watermelon rind

MAKES **1 SERVINGS**

1   cup mixed summer greens and edible flowers

¼   cup Mango-Lime Vinaigrette (recipe follows)

6   thin slices Pickled Watermelon Rind (recipe follows)

3   thin slices Spice Cured Salmon (recipe follows)

Toss greens with Mango-Lime Vinaigrette. Arrange on plate with Pickled Watermelon Rind and Spice Cured Salmon.

Mango Lime Vinaigrette

½   ripe mango, peeled and seeded

1   cup vegetable oil

⅓   cup fresh lime juice

6   tablespoons Lime Simple Syrup (recipe follows)

2   tablespoons minced shallots

1   tablespoon lime zest

¼   teaspoon white pepper

2   teaspoons Chef Paul Prudhomme's Vegetable Magic®

½   teaspoon pink peppercorns

2   tablespoons mirin

Purée mango in blender. Whisk together with remaining ingredients in large bowl.

Lime Simple Syrup

6   tablespoons sugar

¼   cup water

   Zest of ½ lime

Combine all ingredients in a saucepan and bring to a boil, stirring constantly. Cool and set aside.

Pickled Watermelon Rind

1   medium watermelon

2   quarts water

3   cups white vinegar

1¾   cups sugar

4   teaspoons salt

1   tablespoon Chef Paul Prudhomme's Vegetable Magic®

1   teaspoon ground red pepper

½   teaspoon ground cinnamon

1   large (about ¾-pound) onion, julienned

5   ounces jalapeño peppers, cut in quarters

3   ounces garlic cloves, peeled and cut in half

Peel skin from melon. Cut melon into 3-inch wide pieces. Cut out red meat from center of melon leaving about ½ inch attached to rind; reserve red melon meat for another use. Thinly slice rind crosswise.

Combine water, vinegar, sugar, salt, Vegetable Magic and ground red pepper in large pot over high heat. Bring to a boil, stirring frequently to dissolve the sugar and salt. Add sliced rind and simmer over medium heat until the rinds are tender but still crunchy, about 45 minutes. Remove from heat and cool to room temperature. Place rind in large jar or mixing bowl. Stir remaining ingredients into cooking liquid and pour over rind. Refrigerate overnight. Serve cold or at room temperature.

Spice Cured Salmon

1	(2-pound) salmon fillet
½	cup chopped carrots
½	cup chopped celery
½	cup chopped leek
1¼	cups sugar
1	cup Chef Paul Prudhomme's Meat Magic®
6	tablespoons chopped fresh dill

Place salmon fillet skin side down on baking sheet. Combine remaining ingredients in small bowl and mix well. Sprinkle seasonings on salmon until it is very well coated. Cover tightly with plastic wrap and refrigerate for 1 to 3 days.

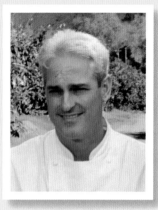

David Reardon

Chef Reardon began his worldwide, whirl-wind career after completing the Sheraton Hotel's Executive Chef Training Program, during which he spent time as the executive chef/direc-tor of culinary ser-vices at The Orchid at Mauna Lani, in Hawaii, as well as the executive chef/food and beverage direc-tor at the Diamond Head Grill in the W Hotel, in Honolulu. He has won numerous honors and awards for his creative and inventive Cal-French creations.

pork scallopini
with lemon caper sauce

MAKES **6 SERVINGS**

12	small (2-ounce) pork scallopini
	Salt and pepper, to taste
¼	cup all-purpose flour
2	eggs, lightly beaten
6	tablespoons clarified butter
1	cup dry white wine
1	cup beef or pork stock
2	tablespoons lemon juice
1	tablespoon grated fresh lemon zest
2	tablespoons capers, rinsed and drained
3	tablespoons cold butter
1	tablespoon chopped fresh parsley

Season pork scallopini with salt and pepper. Dredge in flour, shaking off excess. Dredge in lightly beaten egg. Fry in clarified butter in large skillet over medium-high heat until golden brown. Remove from pan.

Drain drippings from pan and deglaze pan with white wine. Cook until reduced by half and add beef stock. Reduce by half. Add lemon juice, lemon zest and capers. Swirl in cold butter to create an emulsion.

Add chopped parsley and adjust seasoning with salt and pepper to taste. Arrange 2 pork cutlets on each plate and spoon sauce over the top.

pork tenderloin
in citrus-mustard sauce

MAKES **6 SERVINGS**

¼ cup Cara Cara
   Reduction (recipe
   follows)

2 tablespoons honey

¼ cup prepared
   mustard

¼ cup brandy

2 bay leaves

1 rosemary sprig
   Pinch ground red
   pepper

2 pork tenderloins
   (1¼ pounds each),
   trimmed of fat

3 tablespoons clarified
   butter

2 tablespoons minced shallots

1½ cups red wine

2 cups veal stock

3 hot chili peppers, minced
   Salt, to taste

2 tablespoons butter

Roast in preheated 350°F oven about 10 minutes or to desired doneness. Remove from oven and keep warm.

Meanwhile, sweat minced shallots in same skillet over medium heat. Deglaze with wine and cook until reduced to ¼ cup. Add veal stock, chili peppers and reduce to 1 cup. Stir in reserved marinade and bring to a boil, and then reduce heat to simmer. Strain into small sauce pan. Cook over medium heat until sauce thickens slightly. Stir in remaining butter.

Spoon sauce onto 6 plates. Slice pork on a bias and divide among plates, overlapping slices in sauce.

Cara Cara Reduction
   2 cups Cara Cara orange juice (or juice of any navel oranges, or juice from any combination citrus fruits)

Combine Cara Cara Reduction, honey, mustard, brandy, bay leaves, rosemary and red pepper. Pour over pork in resealable food storage bag. Seal bag and refrigerate several hours or overnight.

Remove pork from marinade, reserving marinade. Pat pork dry. Heat clarified butter in skillet and sear pork on all sides. Place pork on rack in roasting pan.

Cook juice in small saucepan over low heat until it has thickened slightly and is reduced to ¼ cup, about 45 minutes to 1 hour.

Saul Romero

Chef Saul Romero is the executive sous chef at the Monterey Plaza Hotel in Monterey, California.

Laura says...

Demi-glace is a rich, concentrated brown stock that is carefully reduced until it becomes a deep, meat-flavored glaze. It can also be found at specialty grocery stores.

pork tri-tip scallopini
with apple cider sauce, potato cakes and sweet and sour cabbage

MAKES **4 SERVINGS**

1	(3-pound) pork tri-tip roast, trimmed of fat
	Salt and pepper, to taste
2	ounces all-purpose flour
2	tablespoons olive oil
4	Potato Cakes (recipe follows)
1	cup Sweet and Sour Cabbage (recipe follows)
2	tablespoons cider vinegar
½	cup apple juice
2	tablespoons minced shallots
¼	cup (½ stick) unsalted butter, cut into small cubes
¾	cup demiglace
¼	cup cognac

Slice pork roast against the grain into ¼-inch-thick pieces. Lightly pound pieces to flatten. Season with salt and pepper, and then dredge in flour and set aside.

Heat olive oil in large skillet over medium heat. Add pork and cook for 3 to 4 minutes per side or to desired doneness.

Place 1 Potato Cake in center of each of 4 plates. Top each Potato Cake with ¼ cup Sweet and Sour Cabbage. Place cooked pork on top of cabbage.

Return skillet to heat and add shallots. Deglaze with cognac (be careful, cognac will flame due to its alcohol content). Add vinegar and apple juice and bring to a boil over high heat. Cook until reduced to about 3 tablespoons then add demiglace. Return to boiling, season with salt and pepper. Remove from heat and whisk in butter, stirring constantly until fully melted. Pour sauce onto plates, drizzling some over each serving of pork.

Potato Cakes

3   russet potatoes
      Salt and pepper, to taste
1   teaspoon ground nutmeg
2   eggs, beaten
½   cup grated Parmesan cheese
¼   cup milk
¼   cup (½ stick) butter, melted

Peel, dry and shred potatoes. Add remaining ingredients and mix well. Pour by scant ¼ cup onto nonstick skillet over medium heat; spread to ½ inch thick. Cook 12 to 14 minutes per side.

Sweet and Sour Cabbage

2   heads red cabbage, shredded
¼   pound green apples, peeled, seeded
      and sliced
2   tablespoons olive oil
¼   cup apple juice
¼   cup raspberry vinegar
2   tablespoons honey
      Brown sugar, to taste
      Salt and pepper, to taste

Cook and stir cabbage and apples in oil over medium-high heat 20 minutes. Add vinegar, apple juice and honey. Turn heat to low. Cook and stir 10 minutes longer. Add brown sugar, salt and pepper.

chili rubbed pork tri-tip
with salad of portofino baby greens, feta cheese and raspberry vinaigrette

MAKES **4 SERVINGS**

1 **(3-pound) pork tri-tip roast, trimmed of fat**
  Chili-Olive Oil Marinade (recipe follows)
2 **bags (6 ounces each) baby greens**
6 **ounces herbed croutons**
6 **ounces feta cheese, cut into ½-inch dice**
½ **cup Raspberry-Mustard Vinaigrette (recipe follows)**

Marinate pork tri-tip in Chili-Olive Oil Marinade about 30 minutes. Discard marinade.

Preheat grill. Grill pork about 6 minutes on each side. Transfer to baking sheet and roast in 350°F oven 10 minutes or to desired doneness. Remove from oven, cover and let rest 5 minutes.

Toss baby greens, croutons and feta with

Raspberry-Mustard Vinaigrette. Cut pork against the grain into ⅛-inch-thick slices. Arrange salad in centers of 4 plates and top with slices of pork. Drizzle vinaigrette on meat and around plate.

Chili-Olive Oil Marinade
1 **tablespoon chili powder**
1 **tablespoon paprika**
1 **tablespoon achiote paste**
1 **tablespoon chopped garlic**
½ **cup olive oil**
¼ **cup lemon juice**
  Salt and pepper, to taste

Combine all ingredients large bowl. Season to taste with salt and pepper. Store in airtight container in refrigerator up to 2 weeks.

Raspberry-Mustard Vinaigrette
2 **tablespoons Dijon mustard**
2 **tablespoons honey**
¼ **cup raspberry purée***
6 **tablespoons rice wine vinegar, divided**
1 **cup olive oil**
  Salt and pepper, to taste

*To make your own fresh raspberry purée, combine 1 ounce of sugar and 1 pound of raspberries in blender. Process until smooth and strain, if desired, through fine mesh strainer.

Whisk together mustard, honey, raspberry purée and 3 tablespoons vinegar. Gradually whip in olive oil. Whip in remaining vinegar and season to taste with salt and pepper.

baby arugula

with heirloom tomatoes, buffalo mozzarella, avocado and white balsamic vinaigrette

MAKES **4 SERVINGS**

3 heirloom tomatoes, each cut into 8 wedges

6 ounces fresh buffalo mozzarella, cut into ¼-inch slices

2 avocados, peeled and sliced

2 bags (5 ounces each) baby arugula

½ cup White Balsamic Vinaigrette (recipe follows)

Arrange 6 tomato wedges, one-fourth sliced cheese and one-fourth avocado slices in a circle on each of 4 plates. Toss arugula with White Balsamic Vinaigrette and season to taste with salt and pepper. Mound dressed arugula in center of plates and serve.

White Balsamic Vinaigrette

1 teaspoon chopped fresh garlic

1 tablespoon chopped shallots

¼ cup honey or sugar

6 tablespoons white balsamic vinegar

¾ cup olive oil

1 tablespoon chopped fresh basil

2 tablespoons lemon juice
Salt and pepper, to taste

Whisk together garlic, shallots, honey and white balsamic vinegar. Gradually whip in olive oil. Season to taste with salt and pepper. Fold in basil and lemon juice.

Carl Schroeder

Chef Carl Schroeder graduated from the Culinary Institute of America, and worked at La Crémaillère in Bedford, New York before moving to California.
He worked on both coasts extensively, including stints at Aqua in San Francisco and at Domaine Chandon in Yountville. In 2002, he opened Arterra Restaurant in the Marriott Del Mar Hotel in Del Mar, California, where he incorporates fresh ingredients into his creative dishes, making it a destination dining spot.

wisconsin gorgonzola soufflé

MAKES **8 SERVINGS**

¼ cup (½ stick) butter
3 ounces all-purpose flour
2 cups cold milk
7 ounces crumbled Gorgonzola cheese
6 eggs, separated
   Salt and pepper, to taste

Melt butter in saucepan over medium heat. Add flour and stir rapidly with a wooden spoon. Cook until light brown. Add cold milk slowly, whisking continually. Cook over medium heat 10 minutes or until sauce is smooth and thick. Remove from heat and whisk in crumbled cheese. Let cool slightly. Whisk in egg yolks 1 at a time. Cool mixture completely. Whip egg whites to soft peak stage. Fold into cooled sauce.

Divide among 8 buttered and floured 2-ounce ramekins. Place in large shallow pan; fill pan with enough hot water to come halfway up side of ramekins. Bake in preheated 300°F oven for 15 to 18 minutes, or until golden brown. Remove ramekins from water bath, reduce oven to 325°F and cook 15 to 20 minutes. Remove from oven; let cool until just warm, and unmold onto buttered parchment paper.

autumn apple salad
with vinaigrette

MAKES **8 SERVINGS**

16 cups mixed salad greens
    Vinaigrette (recipe follows)
2   large Red Delicious apples, cored and
    cut into ½-inch pieces
8   ounces crumbled blue cheese

Add greens to vinaigrette; toss to coat. Divide among plates and top with apple and blue cheese. Serve with Wisconsin Gorgonzola Soufflé.

Vinaigrette
1   tablespoon Dijon mustard
½   cup banyuls vinegar*

1½ cups olive oil
¼   cup chopped fresh parsley
¼   cup chopped fresh tarragon
¼   cup chopped fresh cilantro
¼   cup minced shallots
    Salt and pepper, to taste

Note: Banyuls vinegar is made from a fortified French wine called "Banyuls." If unavailable, substitute another red wine vinegar.

Whisk together mustard and vinegar. Gradually whisk in oil. Add all other ingredients and adjust seasoning with salt and pepper to taste.

brandied apple-stuffed pork

MAKES **4 SERVINGS**

½ cup peeled, diced red apples
2 tablespoons sugar
3 tablespoons brandy
2 tablespoons Dijon mustard
8 boneless pork loin chops (about 5 ounces each)
8 thin slices bacon
Sautéed Swiss Chard (recipe follows)
Roast Maple Sweet Potatoes (recipe follows)
Cider Sauce (recipe follows)

Sauté apples in sugar in skillet over high heat. Deglaze pan with brandy. Let cool then toss with mustard.

Clean pork loin chops. Cut hole in center of chops. Stuff with apples. Wrap bacon around chops, sealing all sides. Roast in 450°F oven 8 minutes or to desired doneness.

Serve alongside Sautéed Swiss Chard. Top pork with Roast Maple Sweet Potatoes and Cider Sauce.

Sautéed Swiss Chard

1 tablespoon vegetable oil
¼ cup chopped onion
1 clove garlic, minced
6 stalks Swiss chard, cleaned and coarsely chopped

Heat oil in skillet; add onion and cook until soft and translucent. Add garlic, being careful not to burn. Add chard and cook until slightly wilted.

Roast Maple Sweet Potatoes

2 large sweet potatoes
3 cups apple juice
3 tablespoons brown sugar
1 tablespoon ground ginger
6 tablespoons maple syrup

Peel sweet potatoes and cut into medium dice. Set aside.

Combine apple juice, brown sugar, ginger and maple syrup in 2-quart saucepan. Cook over medium heat until sugar dissolves.

Place potatoes in roasting pan. Pour sugar syrup over potatoes and bake at 350°F 20 minutes or until potatoes are tender.

Cider Sauce

4 ounces pork scraps (from trimmed roasts and chops)
5 tablespoons finely diced carrots
5 tablespoons finely diced celery
5 tablespoons finely diced onion
1 quart veal stock
6 stems fresh parsley
2 cups apple juice

Heat 2-quart saucepan over medium-high heat until very hot. Add pork scraps and sear until well caramelized. Add carrots, celery and onion and cook 4 minutes, stirring frequently.

Add veal stock and parsley stems. Cook 30 minutes and strain. Return strained liquid and apple juice to saucepan. Cook over medium heat until reduced to half original volume or until thick enough not to run on plate.

Ranier Schwarz

Executive Chef Rainer Schwarz was the chef of Whist Restaurant in the Viceroy Hotel in Santa Monica, California.

Laura says...

There are over 2500 varieties of apples grown in the United States. Try your favorite apples in this recipe.

apple strudel
with vanilla ice cream and crème anglaise

MAKES **6 SERVINGS**

¼ cup rum
1 tablespoon vanilla extract
¼ cup toasted almonds
3 tablespoons raisins
6 tablespoons granulated sugar, divided
    Ground cinnamon, to taste
5 Red Delicious apples, peeled, cored and thinly sliced
    Juice of 2 lemons
6 tablespoons plugra-style butter
6 tablespoons graham cracker crumbs
2 eggs beaten with 1 tablespoon water
¼ cup (½ stick) melted butter
8 sheets phyllo dough
1½ cups vanilla ice cream, divided
1½ cups crème anglaise
6 dried apples
6 fresh mint leaves (optional)
6 vanilla beans, sliced lengthwise (optional)
6 tablespoon powdered sugar (optional)

Combine rum, vanilla extract, almonds, raisins, 4 tablespoons granulated sugar and cinnamon. Add apples and lemon juice and toss to combine. Set aside.

Melt plugra-style butter. Stir in graham cracker crumbs and remaining 2 tablespoons sugar. Cook slowly 2 to 3 minutes until crumbs are toasted and have absorbed all the butter. Stir half crumb mixture into apples.

Layer 4 sheets of phyllo dough, brushing each sheet with melted butter. Arrange one-half of apples to cover one-half of layered phyllo dough. Sprinkle with one-half remaining crumb mixture. Roll tightly,

tucking in ends burrito style. Repeat with remaining 4 layers phyllo dough and remaining apples and crumb mixture.

Bake strudels on parchment-lined baking sheets in preheated 350°F oven 15 minutes. Brush liberally with egg wash and bake 15 minutes more or until golden brown. Transfer on parchment to wire racks and cool until just warm.

Trim ends of strudels and cut each into 3 equal pieces. Serve each portion with ¼ cup ice cream and ¼ cup crème anglaise. Garnish each plate with dried apple, mint leaf, one split vanilla bean and powdered sugar, if desired.

Mark Sherline

Chef Mark Sherline is the executive chef for the Hard Rock Hotel in Las Vegas, Nevada.

tomato and herb salad

with spring mix and goat cheese tart

MAKES **1 SERVING**

6	red cherry tomatoes
6	yellow cherry tomatoes
1	tablespoon chopped fresh basil
1	tablespoon chopped fresh chervil
1	tablespoon chopped fresh tarragon
	Extra-virgin olive oil
	Red wine vinegar
	Salt and pepper, to taste
	Phyllo dough
	Nonstick cooking spray
6	ounces goat cheese
1	tablespoon chopped fresh chives
1	bag (6 ounces) mixed spring greens

Cut cherry tomatoes in half and toss with basil, chervil, tarragon, olive oil, vinegar, salt and pepper; set aside to marinate.

Spread out phyllo dough and cut 5 small (1½-inch) rounds per serving. Spray phyllo rounds with nonstick cooking spray. Bake in preheated 400°F oven 3 to 4 minutes or until golden brown. Cool completely on wire racks.

Whip goat cheese, chives and olive oil until smooth. Spoon 1 teaspoon goat cheese onto each phyllo round, and then stack.

Toss greens with oil and vinegar. Taste and adjust seasoning with salt and pepper. Place tart in center of plate and neatly surround with dressed mixed greens. Arrange cherry tomatoes on greens. Garnish with additional herbs, if desired.

fettuccine and wilted arugula salad
with grilled tiger shrimp

MAKES **1 SERVING**

Extra-virgin olive oil or Truffle-flavored olive oil
Mixed fresh herbs
Salt and pepper, to taste
5   **to 6 (about 1 ounce) tiger shrimp,* peeled and de-veined**
¼   **pound dried fettuccine, cooked according to package directions and kept warm**
1   **bag (6 ounces) baby arugula**
1   **cup julienned red tomato**
1   **cup julienned yellow tomato**
    Grated Pecorino Romano cheese
    Grated zest of 1 lemon

*Shrimp are typically sold according to their size; look for "U-15" shrimp 1 pound of which contains 15 or fewer individual shrimp.

Stir together olive oil, fresh herbs and salt and pepper. Add shrimp and marinate 15 minutes.

Grill shrimp over direct heat about 2 minutes; flip and grill another 2 minutes or to desired doneness.

Toss fettuccine with arugula, julienned tomato, cheese, lemon zest and olive oil, reserving a little tomato, lemon zest and cheese to garnish. Taste and adjust seasoning with salt and pepper.

Spoon pasta into center of plate or bowl and arrange grilled shrimp around it. Drizzle a small amount of olive oil over salad and garnish with reserved tomato, zest and grated cheese.

Carrie Skromme

Executive Pastry Chef Carrie Skromme graduated from the Culinary Institute of America. After working in restaurants, including Lulu's and Stars in San Francisco, and opening Lila's in San Diego, she began teaching at the California School of Culinary Arts in Pasadena. After moving up the academic ladder, she decided to go back into the restaurant industry. She is currently the Executive Pastry Chef for the New York Food Company's Pastry Division.

caramel and candied apples

MAKES **6 TO 8 SERVINGS**

Candied Apples

7½ ounces red candy powder
2½ pounds sugar
1 cup water

Cook ingredients together in large saucepan over medium-high heat until mixture reaches 300°F. Cool slightly; dip apples while still warm. Let set and wrap in plastic wrap or display on platter.

Caramel Apples

1½ pounds caramel
4 ounces white chocolate
1 teaspoon vanilla paste

Cook caramel in microwave or on top of double broiler until soft. Dip apples; cool until caramel sets.

Melt chocolate and stir in vanilla paste. Pipe onto apples in spider web designs. Let set and wrap in plastic wrap or display on a platter.

Chef's Note: Melt 4 ounces milk or bittersweet chocolate in addition to white chocolate and drizzle over apples, too.

ghoulish goodies

MAKES **12 SERVINGS**

12	apples
½	cup lemon juice
2	teaspoons salt
24	whole cloves
48	grains rice

Peel apples and coat with lemon juice and salt. Carve eye sockets, nose and mouth into side of each apple. Pierce each eye socket with a clove and each mouth with 4 grains rice. Dry in warm, well-ventilated spot 2 weeks or place in lower rack of warm oven 2 days.

sour cream apple pie

MAKES **6 TO 8 SERVINGS**

- 1 pound (about 3¼ cups) pastry flour
- 1½ cups (3 sticks) butter
- 1½ teaspoons salt
- ½ cup cold water
- ⅔ cup sour cream
- ⅓ cup plus 3 tablespoons granulated sugar, divided
- 1 egg
  Salt, to taste
- 1 tablespoon vanilla extract
- 3 tablespoons all-purpose flour
- 6 apples, peeled and sliced
- 3 tablespoons brown sugar
- 1 teaspoon ground cinnamon
- ¼ teaspoon ground cardamom

Pulse pastry flour, butter and salt in food processor until mixture forms small clumps. With processor running add just enough cold water for dough to come together. Roll into ball, wrap in plastic wrap and refrigerate 30 minutes. Divide dough in half; roll one half to ⅓-inch thickness and line 10-inch pie plate. Refrigerate remaining dough.

Stir together sour cream, ⅓ cup granulated sugar, egg, a pinch of salt, vanilla extract and all-purpose flour. Stir in apples and pour into pie shell.

Stir together brown sugar, 3 tablespoons remaining granulated sugar, cinnamon and cardamom and sprinkle over filling. Roll out remaining pie dough to ¼-inch thickness and place over filling. Trim edge to ½ inch and crimp decoratively. Cut slit in center of pie to vent steam.

Bake in preheated 350°F oven 1 hour or until juices bubble in center. Once baked, chill pie in freezer 30 minutes to set filling. Serve at room temperature or rewarm.

Video instructions for this recipe are on the companion DVD.

harvest apple cake

MAKES **10 TO 12 SERVINGS**

6 apples, peeled, cored and sliced
2 tablespoons brown sugar
¼ teaspoon ground ginger
1 teaspoon ground cinnamon
½ cup pecans, chopped
½ cup raisins
⅓ cup butter
½ teaspoon salt
1¼ cups granulated sugar
1 cup oil
⅓ cup water
1 tablespoon vanilla extract
4 eggs
3 cups all-purpose flour
1 tablespoon baking powder
1 cup powdered sugar
1 to 2 teaspoons apple cider, divided
Whisk together until smooth

Mix apples, brown sugar, ginger, cinnamon, pecans and raisins until well combined. Set aside.

Beat butter, salt and granulated sugar with electric mixer on high speed 5 minutes. Add oil, water and vanilla and beat until combined; beat in eggs 1 at a time, beating to incorporate each egg. Stop and scrape bowl.

Sift together all-purpose flour and baking powder. Add half dry ingredients to batter and mix 30 seconds to combine. Add remaining dry ingredients and mix on high until incorporated.

Pour half batter into well greased bundt pan (or 13X9-inch pan). Spoon apple filling over batter, and then pour remaining batter over apple filling. Bake in preheated 325°F oven 1 to 1½ hours or until thin knife inserted near center of cake comes out clean. Cool in pan 10 minutes then turn out onto wire rack. Cool completely.

Stir together powdered sugar and 1 teaspoon apple cider; add additional cider as needed to make a smooth glaze. Spoon over cake. Let set 10 minutes before serving.

Lisa Stalvey

Executive Chef Lisa Stalvey began cooking more than 30 years ago. While studying acting, she worked at Good Earth Restaurant, which led to an apprenticeship with Wolfgang Puck. After working at many famous restaurants, she rejoined Wolfgang Puck at Spago in Hollywood. She later alternated between restaurant consulting and working in dining establishments. She has consulted for Paul Newman's company, Newman's Own. She also has created two sauces and written two cookbooks for the company.

meatball seasoned ground beef baked pasta

MAKES 6 TO 8 SERVINGS

1   yellow onion, finely diced
1   tablespoon oil
1½ pounds ground beef
1   tablespoon dried thyme
1   envelope (about 1 ounce) meatball seasoning mix
2   pounds pasta, cooked according to package instructions
1   jar (16 ounces) four-cheese Alfredo-style pasta sauce
1   package (8 ounces) shredded Jack cheese
    Salt and pepper, to taste

Cook onions in oil in large skillet over medium-high heat 5 minutes. Add ground beef, thyme and meatball seasoning. Cook, stirring to break up beef, until no longer pink.

Toss cooked beef with cooked pasta in large bowl to mix well. Stir in Alfredo sauce and shredded Jack cheese. Season to taste with salt and pepper.

Pour into 11X9-inch nonstick pan and bake 8 minutes in preheated 375°F oven.

meatloaf sandwich, french dip style

MAKES **4 SERVINGS**

2 red onions, sliced
2 tablespoons olive oil
1 envelope (about 1 ounce) meatloaf seasoning mix
1 pound ground beef
1 package (8 ounces) provolone or Swiss cheese, sliced
8 slices French bread or sandwich bread
¼ cup honey mustard, divided
Broth (recipe follows)
Black Bean Salad (recipe follows)

Sauté onions in oil in skillet over high heat 10 minutes or until onions are browned. Meanwhile, combine meatlof seasoning and ground beef. Shape into 4 oval patties the size of slices of bread. Grill or sauté to desired doneness.

Spread 1 tablespoon honey mustard on 1 slice bread. Top with 1 cooked patty, one-quarter of cooked onions and 2 slices cheese. Top with another slice bread. Serve with warmed Broth and Black Bean Salad.

Broth
1 can beef broth
1 bottle (10 ounces) Worcestershire sauce

Stir together ingredients in small saucepan over medium heat until warm.

Black Bean Salad
1 can (15 ounces) black beans
1 package (10 ounces) frozen white corn
2 tablespoons sliced red onion
1 tablespoon olive oil
½ cup diced bell peppers, (red, yellow, or green)
½ cup chopped fresh cilantro
½ cup diced green onions
1 tablespoon ground cumin

Combine all ingredients; refrigerate until serving.

fiesta taco burgers

MAKES **4 SERVINGS**

2   **red bell peppers, seeded and sliced**
2   **yellow bell peppers, seeded and sliced**
2   **red onions, sliced**
8   **white mushrooms, sliced**
2   **tablespoons olive oil**
1   **envelope (about 1 ounce) taco**
     seasoning mix
1   **pound ground beef**
    Guacamole (recipe follows)
4   **hamburger buns**
    Queso Ranchero, shredded Jack
     cheese, mayonnaise (optional)

Sauté peppers, onions and mushrooms in oil in large skillet over high heat 5 minutes or until softened and browned. Remove from heat and cool to room temperature.

Mix together taco seasoning and ground beef and shape into 4 patties. Grill or sauté to desired doneness.

Spread 2 tablespoons Guacamole on bottom half of each bun. Top with burgers, sautéed vegetables, and garnish as desired with cheese or mayonnaise.

Guacamole
3   **avocados, sliced**
1   **bunch fresh cilantro, chopped**
    Juice of ½ lime
    Salt and pepper, to taste

Mash avocados with fork. Stir in chopped cilantro and lime juice. Stir in salt and pepper to taste.

Andrew Sutton

Chef Andrew Sutton learned to cook due to family policy: each of the six children in his family was required to prepare dinner one night a week (on the seventh night, they ate out) After training at the Culinary Institute of America he went on to work in award winning restaurants, including Auberge du Soleil restaurant in Napa Valley. While he was there, the restaurant was named "One of the Best Hotel Restaurants" by Condé Nast Traveler.

grilled turkey breast
on a ragù of roast carrots, corn and chanterelle mushrooms with cranberry relish

MAKES **6 SERVINGS**

⅓ cup onions, diced
2 baby carrots, peeled or ¾ cup diced carrots
2 tablespoons butter
⅓ cup cooked and diced bacon
½ cup Merlot
2 cups chicken stock
1 cup chanterelle mushrooms or other mushroom, quartered
1 cup brown chicken "demi-glace"
¾ cup cooked corn
½ cup green beans, cooked and cut into 1-inch pieces
2 tablespoons chopped fresh thyme
2 tablespoons chopped fresh sage
12 (¾-inch-thick) slices honey roasted turkey breast or smoked turkey breast
Vegetable oil
Barbecue spice rub
Prepared cranberry relish
Your favorite dressing (stuffing cooked outside of bird)

Sauté diced onions and carrots in butter until lightly brown, then add bacon. Deglaze with Merlot and reduce by 50%. Stir in chicken stock, mushrooms, demi-glace, corn, green beans, thyme and sage. Cook over low heat until carrots are tender. Ragù can be made up to 1 day in advance, refrigerated and reheated when needed.

Coat turkey breast slices with vegetable oil and rub with barbecue spice rub; set aside to marinate.

Preheat grill to medium-high. Grill turkey 3 minutes per side or until warmed through. Serve over warm ragù in large pasta bowls or chop plates. Serve with cranberry relish and your family's favorite dressing.

holiday citrus turkey salad
with roasted carrot, lime and chile dressing

MAKES **4 TO 6 SERVINGS**

2 cups diced cooked turkey
3 tablespoons olive oil
½ teaspoon lemon zest
½ teaspoon lime zest
½ teaspoon orange zest
½ cup diced red bell peppers
½ cup diced cooked butternut squash
½ cup cooked corn
¼ cup sliced green onions
½ cup diced green apple
½ cup pecan pieces, toasted
2 jalapeño peppers, seeded
2 tablespoons minced fresh cilantro
2 tablespoons minced fresh thyme
1 tablespoon minced fresh sage
2 to 3 avocados, diced (optional)
Salad greens (optional)
½ cup Carrot, Lime and Chile Dressing (recipe follows)

Combine olive oil and zests in small bowl. Marinate diced turkey in zest mixture at least 1 hour.

Toss all salad ingredients except avocado and allow flavors to mix 30 minutes. Serve with avocado slices and salad greens, if desired.

To serve, place turkey salad in cylinder mold in center of plate. Pack turkey with back of a spoon and remove mold.

Carrot, Lime and Chile Dressing

3 to 4 carrots, cut in half
1 tablespoon olive oil
1 teaspoon minced garlic
1 New Mexico chile, seeded
1 Ancho chile, seeded
3 cups chicken stock
¾ cup sour cream
1 tablespoon lime juice
2 tablespoons chopped fresh cilantro
1 tablespoon honey
Kosher salt, to taste

Sauté halved carrots in warm oil saucepan over medium heat until lightly browned on all sides. Add minced garlic and seeded chiles; continue to sauté 3 more minutes. Add chicken stock and bring to a boil. Simmer about 45 minutes or until carrots are tender and liquid has been reduced by half. Place carrots in blender and add sour cream, lime juice, cilantro, honey and salt. Carefully purée mixture until smooth, adjust seasoning and chill. Mixture should be light and creamy, about the consistency of ranch dressing.

Evan Treadwell

Executive Chef Evan Treadwell was raised in Mendocino, California where he learned to cook from his grandmother, a teacher of home economics for more than twenty years. He has studied culinary arts at the Opportunities Industrialization Center West in Menlo Park and at the Culinary Institute of America in St. Helena. His culinary style combines textures and flavors while using classical techniques and fresh regional ingredients, bringing out the best in each dish he prepares.

grilled salmon
with orzo pasta and dijon mustard-olive butter

MAKES **8 SERVINGS**

½ cup (1 stick) butter, softened to room temperature

16 niçoise olives, pitted and chopped

1 medium shallot, chopped

1 tablespoon chopped fresh Italian parsley

2 teaspoons Dijon mustard

3 cups orzo pasta

8 (6- to 8-ounce) salmon fillets (each about 1¼ to 1½ inches thick)

Olive oil, to taste

Whole niçoise olives (optional)

Fresh Italian parsley sprigs (optional)

Mix first 5 ingredients in processor until well blended, but still slightly chunky, occasionally scraping down sides of the bowl. Season to taste with salt and pepper. Transfer to small bowl; cover and refrigerate (may be prepared up to 2 days in advance). Soften slightly to room temperature before using.

Cook orzo in large pot of boiling salted water until tender but still firm to bite. Drain; return to same pot. Keep warm.

Heat grill. Brush salmon fillets with olive oil. Place salmon on grill skin-side up and cook 2 minutes, and then turn 45 degrees and cook 2 more minutes (this creates criss-cross grill marks). Flip salmon over and cook another 3 to 4 minutes or to desired doneness.

Stir half of mustard-olive butter into orzo pasta. Toss to coat. Divide orzo among 8 plates. Top each serving with 1 salmon fillet. Place small dollop of mustard-olive butter atop each salmon fillet. Garnish with whole olives and parsley sprigs, if desired, and serve.

prawn, citrus and green olive salad

with aged sherry vinaigrette

MAKES **8 SERVINGS**

- 1 cup olive oil
- ⅓ cup aged Spanish sherry
- 3 garlic cloves, minced
- 1½ teaspoons sugar
- 2 teaspoons grated orange peel
- 2 oranges, or more as needed
- 1 grapefruit, or more as needed
- 1 pound large prawns, cooked (about 2 dozen total)
- 2 cups green olives, pitted and sliced
- 3 green onions, minced
  Salt and pepper, to taste
- 2 packages (6 ounces each) mixed baby greens

Whisk first 5 ingredients in large bowl for dressing. Using sharp knife, cut and peel white pith from citrus. Working over bowl to catch juices, cut between membranes to release segments into bowl. Continue to create 1 cup orange segments and 1 cup grapefruit segments.

Add olives and prawns; season to taste with salt and pepper. Cover and refrigerate 1 hour. Toss baby greens and vinaigrette in large bowl and mix well. Arrange salad on 8 plates as desired, topping each salad with about 3 prawns.

Philippe Trosch

Executive Chef Philippe Trosch is a native of Biarritz, France. Raised by restaurateur parents, he entered culinary school at the age of 17, and subsequently, enrolled in Cornell University's School of Hotel & Restaurant Management. He worked in such famous kitchens as the Ritz Hotel in London, Michelin's three-star Le Moulin de Mougins, and the Biltmore Hotel in Los Angeles before accepting the position at Tucson's Ventana Room.

seedless grape gazpacho
with tomato and mozzarella

MAKES **4 SERVINGS**

2   pounds seedless white grapes
½   cup water
1   clove garlic
    Salt and pepper, to taste
1   organic tomato
8   ounces fresh mozzarella cheese
4   fresh basil leaves
2   tablespoons olive oil
1   cup seedless black grapes

Wash seedless white grapes. Blend with water and garlic in blender until smooth. Season to taste with salt and pepper. Refrigerate mixture 1 hour.

Peel tomato and cut into 4 thin slices; season lightly with salt and pepper. Cut 8 thin slices of mozzarella cheese and season lightly with salt and pepper.

Layer tomato and mozzarella slices in 4 soup bowls. Divide chilled white grape gazpacho among bowls. Slice seedless black grapes into fourths and place on top of tomato and cheese stacks. Sprinkle with olive oil and top with basil leaves.

romaine salad
with spanish cabra goat cheese and grapes

MAKES **4 SERVINGS**

4   romaine lettuce hearts
¼   pound queso de cabra or other goat
      cheese
¼   cup mixed fresh herbs
8   lemon wedges
½   cup seedless black grapes, quartered
½   cup julienned radishes
4   tablespoons olive oil
      Salt and pepper, to taste

Wash romaine with a little vinegar and water. Trim romaine from top, leaving approximately 3-inch long heart. Place 1 romaine heart on each of 4 plates. Sprinkle with goat cheese and fresh mixed herbs. Garnish with lemon wedges, sliced black grapes and finely chopped radish. Drizzle each salad with 1 tablespoon olive oil, and then salt and pepper to taste.

roasted romaine hearts
with shallot-red wine reduction and shallot olive oil

MAKES **6 SERVINGS**

1   **pound shallots**
½   **cup plus 2 tablespoons olive oil**
1   **bottle Cabernet Sauvignon red wine**
6   **romaine lettuce hearts**
½   **cup (1 stick) butter**
¼   **cup mixed fresh herbs**
    Salt and pepper, to taste

Peel and slice shallots. Divide evenly between 2 saucepans. Pour olive oil into one pan and cook over low heat until shallots are golden. Add red wine to another pan and cook over low heat until reduced to ⅓ original volume (about 1 cup total).

Fill 5-quart saucepan with water. Bring to boil. Wash lettuce with a little vinegar and water. Blanch lettuce in boiling water 1 minute and dry on clean towels.

Melt butter in skillet over medium heat. Add blanched romaine hearts and cook until golden. Place 2 golden hearts romaine lettuce on plate. Dress with red wine reduction and some shallot olive oil. Sprinkle with fresh mixed herbs, and then season to taste with salt and pepper.

James Waller

Chef James Waller began his career in Southern California, where he worked for more than 11 years at the famous Hotel Del Coronado, preparing state dinners for many presidents. For more than 10 years, he has served as the Executive Chef at the Monterey Plaza Hotel & Spa, where he has won the Five Star Diamond Chef award numerous times.

schooner's new england chowder
served in a baked potato shell

MAKES **8 SERVINGS**

2	tablespoons butter
1	onion, diced
1	cup diced celery
1	teaspoon chopped garlic
¼	cup all-purpose flour
¼	tablespoon sherry wine
¼	tablespoon white wine
2	russet potatoes, peeled and diced
¾	cup frozen chopped clams, thawed
2	cups clam juice
1	cup heavy cream
1½	cups milk
3	tablespoons clam soup base
	Black pepper, to taste
	Sherry wine, to taste

Sauté butter, onions, celery and garlic in large skillet over medium-high heat until softened but not browned. Add flour and cook 5 minutes. Deglaze with sherry and white wine and cook 5 more minutes. Add potatoes, clams and clam juice, and bring to a boil. Add cream, milk and clam base. Season to taste with pepper and sherry.

To serve in baked potato shell, microwave medium potato on HIGH 5 minutes. Place in bowl, split open and top with warm chowder.

grilled diver scallops
with grapefruit, avocado and upland cress salad

MAKES **8 SERVINGS**

1	clove garlic, minced
	Juice of 1 lemon
	Salt and pepper, to taste
8	basil leaves, julienned
16	large fresh diver scallops, under-10-per-pound size (about 1½ pounds)
3	large Texas pink grapefruits, cut into 24 segments
2	avocados, peeled and cut into quarters, tossed in a little grapefruit juice to keep from turning brown
24	grape tomatoes, cut in half
2	bunches watercress, trimmed

Combine garlic and lemon juice in small bowl. Blend with hand mixer and slowly add enough oil to emulsify. Season with salt and pepper, and stir in basil. Set aside.

Season scallops well with salt and pepper. Sear in very hot skillet pan. Place in 375°F oven to finish cooking. Scallops should be firm and juicy when done.

Toss grapefruit, avocado, tomatoes, watercress and dressing together in large bowl. Divide among 8 plates and top each serving with 2 scallops.

grilled kauai shrimp and monterey crab cake
with grilled green garlic and grape tomato jus

MAKES **8 SERVINGS**

24 shrimp, 21-to-25-per-pound size, peeled and deveined
Salt and pepper, to taste
¾ cup (1½ sticks) unsalted butter
32 green garlic cloves, peeled and cooked in chicken stock until soft
2 tablespoons chopped shallots
Juice of 2 lemons
¼ cup Chardonnay wine
1 cup fish stock
2 tablespoons chopped fresh tarragon
36 grape tomatoes
8 Crab Cakes (recipe follows)

Season shrimp with salt and pepper. Sauté in butter over very high heat. Add green garlic and shallot. Cook a few minutes and deglaze with lemon juice and Chardonnay. Remove shrimp and set aside.

Add fish stock to skillet and reduce until slightly thickened. Add tarragon and tomatoes. Cook to heat tomatoes. Season to taste with salt and pepper. Return shrimp to pan and heat through. Place Crab Cakes on 8 plates and top with shrimp. Drizzle sauce on plates around Crab Cakes.

Crab Cakes

1 pound Dungeness crab meat, cleaned and picked
½ red onion, finely chopped
2 ribs of celery, washed and finely diced
3 green onions, cleaned and minced
2 eggs, beaten
½ cup mayonnaise
3 tablespoons chopped fresh parsley
1 teaspoon seafood seasoning blend
3 dashes hot pepper sauce
1 cup bread crumbs
¼ cup (½ stick) unsalted butter

Combine all ingredients except bread crumbs and butter; fold until batter holds together.

Form into 8 cakes, and coat both sides with bread crumbs.

Melt butter in pan over medium heat, and fry cakes on both sides until lightly browned.

Stephen Window

Executive Chef
Stephen Window
attended culi-
nary school near
his hometown of
Manchester, England.
He worked in some
of the most presti-
gious restaurants
in England before
moving to the South
Pacific where he
developed his style
of combining Asian
ingredients with
fresh products. Chef
Window cooked pro-
fessionally in the U.S.
and the Philippines
before he moved to
La Jolla and opened
Roppongi. Chef
Window has had the
honor of cooking at
the James Beard
House twice.

tiger shrimp skewers
with tomato-horseradish-nectarine salsa

MAKES **4 SERVINGS**

4	nectarines
¼	pound fresh tomatoes, skinned and finely chopped
1	tablespoon chopped fresh cilantro
½	tablespoon rice wine vinegar
1	tablespoon simple syrup
	Salt and pepper, to taste
1	tablespoon wasabi powder
1	tablespoon water
	Juice of 1 lemon
1	cup ketchup
1	tablespoon grated fresh horseradish
16	tiger shrimp, 13-to-15-per-pound size, deveined
2	tablespoons extra-virgin olive oil
1	tablespoon sesame seeds

Dice nectarines. Combine with tomatoes, cilantro, vinegar and simple syrup. Season with salt and pepper and allow to marinate 2 hours.

Stir wasabi powder into water, and then stir in lemon juice, ketchup and horseradish. Set aside until needed.

Skewer shrimp through tail and up through the back. Season with salt and pepper and brush with olive oil. Grill over direct heat on open grill, turning frequently.

Sprinkle shrimp with sesame seeds and serve with salsa and tomato horseradish.

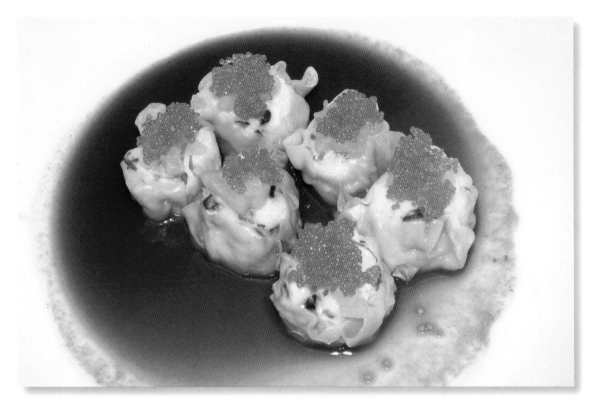

peach lobster shu mai
with shiitake mushrooms and tobiko caviar

MAKES **4 SERVINGS**

1	(1½-pound) Maine lobster
¼	cup chopped fresh chives
¼	cup julienned Thai basil
1	tablespoon fish sauce
	Salt and pepper, to taste
¼	cup finely chopped shallots
1	tablespoon extra virgin olive oil
½	cup white wine
1	cup lobster essence
½	cup thinly sliced shiitake mushrooms
2	tablespoons butter
2	peaches, skinned, peeled, and diced
16	shu mai wrappers
1	tablespoon tobiko caviar

Poach lobster in rapidly boiling salted water for 2 minutes. Remove from boiling water and cool. Remove all meat from lobster, chop finely and mix with chives, basil and fish sauce; season with salt and pepper to taste.

Sauté shallots and lobster shells in oil. Add basil stalks, white wine and lobster essence. Reduce and strain; set aside for later.

Sauté shiitake mushrooms in butter in same pan. Allow to cool. Add to lobster mixture and fold in peaches.

Divide mixture between shu mai wrappers and fold to close. Steam in bamboo steamer basket. Remove to serving platter and top with caviar and lobster reduction.

Tim Woods

Chef Tim Woods was the principal chef and master gardener at Echo Restaurant in Fresno, California. His style of cooking is a combination of California cuisine and classic French cuisine. On a daily basis, Woods collects the freshest ingredients from his garden and local proprietors and creates a menu around them.

Laura says...

In Italy the word "prosciutto" is often used to mean any kind of ham. "Prosciutto" comes from the Italian verb "prosciugare," which means "to dry."

pickled peaches
with prosciutto appetizer

MAKES **4 SERVINGS**

1	cup sugar
½	cup white wine vinegar
½	cup champagne
4	large peaches, peeled, pitted and sliced into eighths
¼	pound imported prosciutto, sliced paper thin

Heat sugar, vinegar and champagne in medium saucepan over medium heat until boiling. Pour over peaches in a large bowl. Cool to room temperature. Pickled peaches can be refrigerated for 4 to 5 days.

Divide prosciutto among 4 plates. Top prosciutto with peaches. Fold edges of prosciutto up and over peaches. Serve immediately.

peach cobbler

MAKES 2 SERVINGS

2½   pounds peaches, peeled and sliced
2¾   cups flour, divided
½   cup sugar, divided
1   tablespoon plus 1 teaspoon baking powder
¼   cup butter
¼   cup heavy cream

Toss peaches with 1 tablespoon flour and 1 tablespoon sugar. Pour into pie plate.

Mix remaining flour, remaining sugar and baking powder in large bowl. Cut butter into flour mixture with hands until it is the texture of cornmeal. Pour in cream and stir just until combined. Shape into patties the size of silver dollars. Place dough on top of peaches in pie plates. Bake in preheated 375°F oven 40 to 45 minutes or until golden brown.

poached peaches in bitter almond syrup
with buttermilk blue cheese

MAKES 4 SERVINGS

2   cups water
1   cup sugar
8   peach kernels (crack peach pit and remove kernel)
4   peaches, peeled and sliced in half
¼   pound buttermilk blue cheese

Combine water, sugar and peach kernels in medium saucepan. Simmer over medium heat 7 to 8 minutes. Reduce heat.

Add peeled peaches to syrup. Poach 5 to 6 minutes on low heat. Remove with a slotted spoon. Allow to cool. Serve with blue cheese crumbled on top.

index

METRIC CONVERSION CHART

VOLUME MEASUREMENTS (dry)

$^1/_8$ teaspoon = 0.5 mL
$^1/_4$ teaspoon = 1 mL
$^1/_2$ teaspoon = 2 mL
$^3/_4$ teaspoon = 4 mL
1 teaspoon = 5 mL
1 tablespoon = 15 mL
2 tablespoons = 30 mL
$^1/_4$ cup = 60 mL
$^1/_3$ cup = 75 mL
$^1/_2$ cup = 125 mL
$^2/_3$ cup = 150 mL
$^3/_4$ cup = 175 mL
1 cup = 250 mL
2 cups = 1 pint = 500 mL
3 cups = 750 mL
4 cups = 1 quart = 1 L

VOLUME MEASUREMENTS (fluid)

1 fluid ounce (2 tablespoons) = 30 mL
4 fluid ounces ($^1/_2$ cup) = 125 mL
8 fluid ounces (1 cup) = 250 mL
12 fluid ounces (1$^1/_2$ cups) = 375 mL
16 fluid ounces (2 cups) = 500 mL

WEIGHTS (mass)

$^1/_2$ ounce = 15 g
1 ounce = 30 g
3 ounces = 90 g
4 ounces = 120 g
8 ounces = 225 g
10 ounces = 285 g
12 ounces = 360 g
16 ounces = 1 pound = 450 g

DIMENSIONS

$^1/_{16}$ inch = 2 mm
$^1/_8$ inch = 3 mm
$^1/_4$ inch = 6 mm
$^1/_2$ inch = 1.5 cm
$^3/_4$ inch = 2 cm
1 inch = 2.5 cm

OVEN TEMPERATURES

250°F = 120°C
275°F = 140°C
300°F = 150°C
325°F = 160°C
350°F = 180°C
375°F = 190°C
400°F = 200°C
425°F = 220°C
450°F = 230°C

BAKING PAN SIZES

Utensil	Size in Inches/Quarts	Metric Volume	Size in Centimeters
Baking or Cake Pan (square or rectangular)	8×8×2	2 L	20×20×5
	9×9×2	2.5 L	23×23×5
	12×8×2	3 L	30×20×5
	13×9×2	3.5 L	33×23×5
Loaf Pan	8×4×3	1.5 L	20×10×7
	9×5×3	2 L	23×13×7
Round Layer Cake Pan	8×1½	1.2 L	20×4
	9×1½	1.5 L	23×4
Pie Plate	8×1¼	750 mL	20×3
	9×1¼	1 L	23×3
Baking Dish or Casserole	1 quart	1 L	—
	1½ quarts	1.5 L	—
	2 quarts	2 L	—